Key to the Spirit World

or
The Art of Living

Johann Baptist Krebs

Key to the Spirit World

or
The Art of Living

Johann Baptist Krebs

translated by Kerry A Nitz

K A Nitz
WHANGANUI, NEW ZEALAND

Schlüssel zur Geisterwelt, oder Die Kunst des Lebens
published in German 1833
under the pseudonym J. Kernning

This translation into New Zealand English
Copyright © K A Nitz 2025
All rights reserved

ISBN: 978-0-473-73413-8

Table of Contents

Translator's Note 7
Foreword 9
Entrance 11
Destiny of the Human 15
Spirit World 17
Present 21
Krz 23
Retrospective 33
Glances into the 17th Century 35
New Acquaintance 37
L...h's Doubt 53
Second Visit 55
Third Visit 63
New Acquaintance 69
L...h as Student 77
L...h in H...g 87
L...h as Helper 89
L...h by the Sickbed 93
The Interrupted Suicide 97
Public Works 103
Retrospective 121
A Glance into the 13th and 14th Centuries 125
The Family Er..k..ng 127
The New Chaplain 133
Gottfried von Er..k..ng 137
The Instruction 141
Germany 151
Gottfried's First Deed 153
New Enemies 157
New Battle 163
Gottfried's Homecoming 167
The Townsmen 169
Order Chapter 173
Overview 177

Translator's Note

For the English translation of Bible texts I have made use of the King James Version. Where I thought it would be helpful I have also inserted missing Biblical citations in the footnotes.

The occasionally somewhat idiosyncratic approach of the author to presenting dialogue has also been retained in part.

***

Foreword

The age desires to be informed about the nature of the spirit world, for it has been spoken and written about for years. How insufficient the utterances of the somnambulists and the ghost visions of the neurasthenic girls and women are, we learn daily, for no positive truth emerges from all their phenomena and explanations. None of all their performances rises above their limited opinions and above the prejudices of the region and place. For this reason the author saw himself caused to illuminate the matter more closely and to consider it from a standpoint where the laws of reason do not suffer hardship, but rather obtain a higher sphere for their activity.

The historical form which was chosen for this task seemed in every respect to be the most expedient, because history, in that it stands there as explicable allegory, gives at the same time a testimony to the characteristics present and the possibilities for their use. The events are drawn from safe sources and leave no doubt in respect to their truthfulness. Even the doctrines which lead to the proposed goal find themselves woven into those histories, and we give them to the reader thus more overtly than permitted for a doctrine which can only be fully comprehended through practise.

The truth is to be found everywhere, when you separate the impure and merely accidental from the essential and necessary, and in this way consider a matter in its inner and positive peculiarity. The essays and events of the book have been regarded and recorded in this sense, and we wish that they might scatter seeds by which better fruits are made ripe than have sprouted from the treatments of the visionaries and dreamers.

Johann Baptist Krebs

It is not the intention here to rebuke or jump ahead, it is merely about pure, spiritual truth and in what way this happens must be all the same if only the goal is reached. But truth is only possible if the one who seeks to share it with others has felt it themselves and stands at the level where the phenomena of the spirit world reveal themselves and give him materials for new concepts and forms of thought. The pure truth demands the highest immediacy; only the open ear can perceive the harmony of the notes, only someone who has had experiences in the realm of the spirit themselves can establish principles about it, and so this little work appears both for reference and even more for the instruction of those who are serious about becoming clear about the goal of human life.

The author.

Entrance

"Keys to the spirit world". The task is set, let us see whether and how it is to be solved.

Is there a spirit world? Many ask this. The earth goes about the sun and about its axis; the uneducated does not believe it — for it argues against the senses. There is a spirit world. The enlightened, worldly human, the human who is caught up in the whirl of business does not believe it — for it argues against the senses, or as you say, against reason.

Is reason the supreme judge for all aims of the human, or must you, in order to obtain certain information about the spirit world, turn to a different seat of judgement?

To answer this question, we must consider the human race in its beginnings and its present condition.

Over the beginnings of humanity there are two sorts of views which directly contradict each other. The first considers the human in his origins to be a sort of animal, gifted with the abilities of speech and experience. By that he consolidates the received impressions, passed them on to his offspring, who enrich them with new experiences, reproducing from generation to generation, until finally humanity achieves the highest state, similarity to God. According to the second view the human emerges perfect, in divine perfection, from the hand of the creator; what he wishes and needs is placed in his heart, and he knows only the single goal, to fulfill his destiny and to be happy through knowledge of God. If we now see the human differently, then he has lost his way and distanced himself from his sublime, natural state.

The first view has much probability for itself, and the doctrine of the day strengthens it. But if we consider history, phenomena strike us which we cannot unite with the course of this progress. According to all the relics, Egypt was standing at the highest peak of culture, now it has sunken into barbarism. The artistic monuments of Greece are of a sort that, if such a progress were to take place amongst the human race, the art would have to have reached such a height as satisfied all that the boldest fantasies were permitted to wish and the most purified tastes were permitted to expect! But we see in history an eternal rising and falling in all branches of knowledge of the peoples, and can draw from that the conclusion with some certainty that the culture of the human has its given stage which, even if seldom reached, cannot be overstepped in its effects.

What now is the highest point, the highest stage of the human? If we look around ourselves, then you will be tempted to believe we have reached the peak; but behind us, that is, in the past, we discover events which we do not grasp with the usual powers of understanding and are required to either deny them, or to judge them with a yardstick before whose size we feel dizzy.

We see from everything that the doctrine of an eternal forward progress has no firm basis, and therefore pass over to the second view in order to examine what materials it provides us for our task.

The human emerged in the highest perfection from the hand of the creator, and has through false aims and self-made doctrine divided himself from his primal state which set for him the communion with God and all the spirits as his life's goal.

All the books of wisdom are in agreement with this stepping backwards, even the holiest book, the Bible. This has the human in Paradise commit the first sin and lose his heavenly residence. The first offspring of that first created one still have traces of divine purity which lends them such life powers that the later offspring consider them to be wonders. Indeed, we find all nations in their beginnings at the purest and most perfect. A sort of world of giants is shown there unanimously which by and by goes astray, and finally sinks into a state of helplessness in which no trace of the first power and of the true calling is to be found anymore.

What party must we join in order to seek the key to the spirit world? The truthful one is the answer.

Entrance

Question: Which is the truthful?
Answer: The second.
Q: Why the second?
A: Because it alone resolves all the contradictions which we see in the human race.
Q: In what way does it resolve them?
A: It shows us that the human is the most perfect of all created beings, but points at the same time to powers which stand over him and from which he has received his glorious characteristics.
Q: What sort of powers are they?
A: Primal, eternal powers which are originating in nature, and have united in the human into a source of knowledge for the past, present, and future.
Q: These answers are leading even more deeply into the labyrinth and increasing the obstacles to finding the desired key. How should you search?
A: With open mind, open heart, in the thought which streams from life and not from empty hypotheses. There is a spirit world which opens up to everybody who seeks without inhibition, who is not blinded by the darkness of book learning and self-made virtue.
Q: How can you escape this blindness?
A: If the human considers himself to be an independent creature which has its own, free knowledge, and does not have to first seek with others the goal of his existence.
Q: How is this free state to be obtained?
A: Through self-use of your powers, through looking within into your life's most secret workshops, and through the recognition of the effects which arise from it.

***

Destiny of the Human

Animals and plants achieve the highest goal which is set for them; but we see the human in confusion. Is this supposed to be the plan of creation in order to purify him through the urge to doubt and struggles and all the more cleanly bring him to the goal? Or is there a primal state which leads him, like it happens with animals and plants, to the highest goal of his existence? When we examine this question, we come closer to our goal, and the hope of unlocking the spirit world gains in strength.

There must be a primal state of the human which, if he does not abandon the correct path, directs him to his destiny.

What is the destiny of the human?

Is it the connecting to the world of desires, to the bustle of the day, to sorrows and worries, to struggle and fears, to the many-sidedness of our wishes, to all the trouble which meets us and nowhere allows us a resting point? That cannot be, otherwise the human would be the poorest of all the creatures and would have to languish in constant grief when all of nature was rejoicing.

The destiny of the human is of a spiritual nature and can therefore not be reached in the visible. The thought is the purest characteristic of life and we are required to consider it as the basis of destiny. In the human it is perfectly present, for it comprises past, present, and future; it measures at the same time space in all relationships, and adds itself by these characteristics to the infinite.

Which of these characteristics is the most important for the human? In which does he find contentment and calm? The past illuminates him, but fills him at the same time with ever new wishes. The present besieges him, and bars to him the path to freedom and to happiness in that it places him in the struggle with all the elements. Space is a great pantry in which we observe the phenomena of creation, but never obtain a goal. In the future lies our wishes, in it alone can the aim of our existence unfold and be fulfilled. The past has no charm when the future is draped with storm clouds. The present is empty and depressing without prospect of a future. Space can offer us nothing at all if it is not pointing to the future. The future is the goal of the human! To establish a free, invincible existence is his sole striving, his morals and his destiny.

Good! To the future we want to turn, it shall open up for us, then we will have obtained the goal after which everyone, great and small, rich and poor, are yearning.

But how can we recognise that which is closed off to the natural sight, where the sound of the voice is not enough, that which no learnedness can decipher and no force can open. Here we enter into a realm of new powers which flow from another source than we see in the usual tumult of the day. Here we place ourselves on the threshold of the spirit world which we feel disposed to unlock.

The human is born for this spirit world; it is his goal, and only in hit can he reach what his soul desires — an abiding existence, in uninterrupted peace.

Eternal persistence in the most blessed pleasure of life is therefore the destiny of the human which he can only seek and find in the spirit world.

***

Spirit World

Spirit world, you come closer to us and become more precious to us, for in you our life hopes shall be fulfilled.

The human can outside himself not penetrate within himself, he must go within himself and there listen to his spirit. But where do we find examples which teach us how this looking inside oneself is possible and what results it brings?

Much has already been written about it, but even when the demonstrations are yet so clever and concise, they go without effect past the ears of the human because he cannot take anything fully within himself which is not based on perceptions.

Good! Examples of such perceptions will lead us quicker to the goal than all the explanations of is and is-not.

The first thing which hits our eyes in this respect is the magnetism* which puts the treated person in a state which is directly contrary to the external life of the senses. They hear, see, and feel in the inner-being without the external organs being touched in the slightest. The phenomena are of a purely spiritual nature, and serve us as proof that the human is capable of yet another life than we usually see.

Two egos show themselves with the magnetised person, an outer and an inner. When the outer stops being active, the inner steps into action, and vice versa; when the inner is not working, the outer senses open.

Here is not the place to judge the worth of magnetism as it is dealt with in our day; only so much is to be remarked, that

---

*   [Tr.: an early form of hypnotism.]

it stands there still extremely imperfect because we observe its phenomena only in the sick and the weak.

When the time comes where the man is placed in the magnetised state, then we can expect discoveries which will leave all the current ones far behind.

The man is born to shine, in him the dignity of humanity must be produced, and this is only possible if he achieves that spiritual state in which he can experience and impart the conditions of life.

Still more! The man as independent power on which no other can act on anymore must put himself into the state of the one who is magnetised and must be able to free himself from it as the circumstances demand; only then is he in the position of comparing one with the other and making a safe judgement.

Now it is to be asked whether it would not be possible to imagine the magnetised state as enduring, so that the human would think and decide with his inner ego, and the outer used only for coarse artifices? Such a life view would place us at a standpoint where some phenomena are explained which we cannot analyse with the usual book learning. Indeed, the human would stand in this way there entirely as his own species whose needs arise from the spirit and for whom the animal nature serves as underlay in order to work his spiritual powers on it.

Here we are at the point where so many fall into confusion because they are all too distant from that state, and nonetheless the unveiling of all the secrets to which history points us, and which raise the Bible to a divine book, rests on the assumption of it.

What else did Christ teach us, but to come into the spirit and to win back the lost paradise? That state is spirit and — is the lost paradise. To be in the spirit, to come into it, to live in it, they are the descriptions of all those enlightened men who with the powers of their inner life saw clearly the creation and looked into the future.

Abraham recognises at once the angel and speaks with it. His usual life was the inner, he only walked outwardly when the needs of the day demanded it.

Moses and Elijah spoke with God and lived only in him; hence no event in the external world could surprise them and sadden their inner-being.

The story of Adam is only to be explained clearly and naturally in this way. His life was a constant clairvoyance until, blinded by arrogance, he wanted to know and decide for himself.

In the spirit alone resides the secure life, because it is in everlasting agreement with the primal power, draws from this directly its knowledge, and obtains strength for actions which are inexplicable to the common eye.

Hercules acted in the power of the spirit. Samson struck the Philistines, strengthened by the spirit. Gideon led into battle three hundred against a hundred thousand and destroyed them, because he was in the spirit for which the external world is only dust and chaff in the wind.

When we consider all these phenomena, we must confess that we are far distant from the realm of the spirits, and still have many steps to climb until we can use the key to which this section points.

The human has two egos, an outer and an inner. With the latter he went from the hand of the creator, the former was given to him by the world; and how mightily this works on him can be concluded from that most humans have no trace, even no idea of an inner, spiritual, and free life anymore.

The human has lost his way, distanced himself from the light, and as much as all religions call out to him in vain, "change your ways", he does not hear and runs ever further from his goal.

Spiritual life is the aim of all religions. But religion is necessary so that the human has a signpost to arrive again in his primal state.

The doctrine is given; in that we point to this, we want to clearly see the history of the present and past, encourage those who are lost with lively examples to believe in a higher life, and to return again to themselves, to their innermost ego.

***

Present

If we had not had magnetism, then the present would be poor in spiritual phenomena. But to this, as imperfect as it also is, we owe the nearest proof that there is an inner life in which the spirit world reveals itself.

To the quiet researcher there indeed appear aside from the magnetic treatments yet many instructive features of spiritual life, but these are so hidden and keep their fortune so secret that blatant curiosity perceives nothing of it, and only with timidity do I dare to give a few historical facts which have a connection to our subject.

***

Krz.

In O—w—d it occurred several years ago that Krz., a wealthy retailer, wanted to consign his son, with the agreement of the family, to studies.

Bernhard, as the son was called, became embarrassed over the proposal, asked his parents to refrain from it and to allow him to learn the craft of joinery.

Extremely astonished over this wish, the parents declared themselves directly against it, in that they considered him to be childish. "If you do not want to become a scholar," his father continued; "then dedicate yourself to the trade and I will look after founding an establishment for your future. But for a craft we will never give permission, because it would distance you to much from us."

The son stuck to his plan and said, "Forgive me, dear parents, that I must be disobedient to you! What I desire does not come from me, but rather from a power which commands me and which I must not oppose."

Set more and more in astonishment, they pressed to discover the cause of his refusal. "I must not," he answered; "but when the time comes to talk, then you will approve my behaviour and happily fulfill my wish to become a craftsman."

After twelve days he asked his father and mother to come with him alone into a room. Here he revealed to them that he had concourse with spirits. The parents were startled, but he said, "Be calm and do not have any fear! What I am, I became through you; you have taught me to seek the spirit and to fear the Lord. He has heard me and begrudged to me to look over into his eternal realm where certain calm and blessedness is. From there I was commanded to avoid all learnedness and to become a simple craftsman."

The parents listened to him almost with horror, and believed him in part, also in part not. They advised him to refrain from such things, because a young fellow, like he was, could not distinguish the snares of Satan from the truth. They instructed him to go to the pastor and to speak with him over the matter. But he cried out, "For God's sake! Reveal to no one what I have said here, but hear my request and let me live with the higher command so that you and I do not become unhappy."

The parents stood back, indeed unhappily, from their plan, and allowed him after constant requests to enter into an apprenticeship with a joiner.

The apprenticeship passed by. According to the tradition of the craft the son insisted on going abroad. The mother was startled over this decision and asked him to refrain from it, because already some had become masters without a journey. "Banish every fear," the son said to her; "nothing will happen to me, and as a sign that I speak the truth, I tell you, I will arrive in B..., and live and work there in F...r street, Nro..., with nice people."

The mother looked at him in shock and replied, "How can you speak thus! Wanting to know in advance what happens, is that not called tempting God?!" The son gave her the answer, "Be calm, mother; I love God. He is with me, and it is he who will protect me."

The time for departure came. The father offered him money for it, but he only took a small part of it, in that he said, "As much as I need for the journey and just as much I will bring back again to my father's house."

Accompanied by good wishes, he left his father's house, arrived safely at the place, and encountered everything as he foretold.

He lived to begin with calmly in the house of his master, loved by all and respected because of his industry. Only already after half a year, temptations were appearing in his path which were embittering his stay.

One evening, when he went outside the gate in order to perform an urgent business, he was wanting at the finish of it to return to the town when several of the journeymen of his guild came to him and called upon him to go with them into the tavern. Krz. sought to decline this imposition and pleaded business as an excuse. They did not listen and called as one, "Come along, come along! We must drink to brotherhood." — "We are all brothers," Krz. said, "but I will not go into the tavern." — "What, you coward?", one of them cried; "You must, if you're not a scoundrel!" — "I won't go!", he said somewhat heatedly. — "You must!", they all shrieked and seized him in order to drag him away with themselves. "That is too much," he said; "Let me go or you will suffer." — They laughed at this threat and continued hauling him. At once he stood still and threw everyone who was holding him away from himself with such force that they thought they had been hit by lightning. He continued calmly on his way home, but the others made their snide remarks and suggested you could also visit the tavern without him and have some fun.

Thus it also happened, they drank their fill with strong beer and made a din until deep into the night; but he thanked God that he freed him from this company.

The event became known and steered attention to him from various sides. The one wanted to make his suspect to his master; another conceived stories to damage his good reputation; a third undertook to abuse him in public on the street. He indeed noticed it, but paid it no attention. But when the master made him explain himself and asked for information about various rumours which had reached his ears, he said, "I have gone to work for you and honestly fulfilled what I promised. If you are concerned about me, then I owe you thanks; but if you consider me to be dishonest, then let me leave your house in which I enjoyed myself; that which brought me to you will also further provide for me."

Everyone in the house took his part and asked the master not to let him go. He said, "There is no talk of going away, but rather of envious gossip into which I would like to inquire in order to bring the evil tongues to fall silent." Krz. responded, "You mean well and hence I will stay; but I foresee that here I will have no rest anymore and before four weeks have passed I will be forced to leave you."

The master thought this was a joke and suggested that he would also have a word to say about that. With renewed vehemence the journeymen pursued him and created such a nuisance that in the end the police had to step in-between. They recognised Krz. as the cause of all the disturbances, and although no blame was found on his part, they nevertheless gave him the instruction to leave the town within twenty four hours and to not return again before a year had passed.

When he came home from the interrogation, he said to the master, "Now what I foretold has happened; between today and tomorrow I must leave, and tomorrow is the last day of the third week."

The master made all possible objections to this decision, only it was no help, and when his journeyman went away, he offered him his hand heartily, and said, "Then go with God! You have become dear to me; do not forget us wherever you get to in the world."

Our joiner now made his way on foot, and not until before the gate did he consider: where to? He had heard many good things about the town of M... in respect to his profession, and made the decision to make his way there.

The first days he was entirely alone; half way, however, a wandering journeyman smith joined with him whom he could not be rid of anymore. As pleasant to others company may be, he would have preferred to remain alone in order to dwell undisturbed on his inner doings and thinking. Now he grinned and bore it, and when he noticed that his travel companion was not as well provided for in his pocket, he supported him and usually let him sleep in his room.

When they saw the towers of M..., his comrade cried out with a sigh, "If only heaven provides me with work there! I am not accustomed to travelling so poorly, and I do not like to fall heavily on my parents. If I find no job there, then I do not know how it will go for me further." Our joiner reassured him with the words, "Take heart, you will find work. Pay attention to what I tell you. In D—er Street there is a large smithy; go there, ask to speak to the master, and tell him you are from Bremen, and he will give you a job."

The smith looked at him in astonishment and responded, "You speak as if it were already arranged. How can you know that? Were you already in M...? Do you know that master?"

Krz. responded, "I have never been in M..., do not anyone there either, only just do what I told you and it will not fail you. I myself will also linger in M..., and indeed only two streets across from you. If you are clever, then you will have good days there; but if you cannot control your tongue, then we will both travel on in a quarter of a year."

The smith, full of astonishment, asked incessantly: How? When? Why? But the joiner told him to calm down and to not speak about such things unnecessarily.

"Only explain one thing to me", the journeyman smith asked; "why should I tell my future master my birthplace first?" Krz. replied, "That I will tell you. He worked during his time as a journeyman in Bremen, was terribly sick, and because the craft took such active care of him, out of thankfulness he gives every journeyman who was born there work when it is possible for him."

The journeyman smith received in the vicinity of his prophetic travelling companion a strange feeling; but he decided to make the attempt.

Arriving in M..., he found it as Krz. had foretold. The latter also entered employ, and several weeks passed before they saw each other again; only an unforeseen occurrence led them unexpectedly together.

The magnetism, which at the time was finding adherents and admirers in all the towns of Germany, had spread there too. Two skilled doctors were making every effort to put it to use with the sick in order to expand their knowledge through the state of clairvoyance and to discover new remedies for the suffering of humanity. It happened accidentally that in the family of the master smith a somnambulist was drawing the curiosity of the town to herself. The new journeyman heard about these wonders, and recalled at the same time his strange travelling companion. When they had exhausted themselves one evening in telling stories, he also betrayed his travel adventure, and told of how his companion had foretold for him everything and this had come about in the most wondrous way. The master smith, who heard of it, shared it with the doctor, and the latter, full of the desire to get to know such a travelling sleepwalker, did not tarry in making his acquaintance in order to obtain new information from him.

One morning, as our joiner was busy with difficult work, his master entered the workshop with the doctor. The latter approached him, and asked him from where in the land, and since when the gift had come to him of announcing to others their fate in advance.

The one questioned was embarrassed and asked to be spared such questions because he did not like to speak of things which he considered to be a gift from heaven. The doctor, made even more curious by this answer, did not let off pressing him, and asked the master finally to be permitted to speak with the journeyman in a secluded room. The master complied with this request, and when the two found themselves alone, the following conversation began.

Doctor: "Did you foretell for the journeyman smith that he would find work here?"

Joiner: "Yes."

Doctor: "You also gave him the means whereby he could achieve his wish?"

Joiner: "Yes."

Doctor: "From where did you know that everything would come true?"

Joiner: "I saw it."

Doctor: "This answer does not suffice it. How was it possible for you to see such a thing?"

Joiner: "Am I obliged to tell you that?"

Doctor: "If you possess the love of humanity, yes."

Joiner: "I love humans, and from love for them I stay silent about some things."

Doctor: "If that which you know is good, then you are wrong to be silent."

Joiner: "That may be. I follow my feelings; these do not deceive me in other things, thus I consider them also here to be truthful."

Doctor: "The good is a property of humanity, and nobody may keep it for themselves alone. Hence I ask you to reveal to me with what powers you are seeing into the future."

Joiner: "Inner senses open themselves to me when I am in some embarrassment. With these, I see, hear, and feel what is useful for me and others."

Doctor: "With what means do you open your inner senses?"

Joiner: "To say this would lead us too far, for it is tied to the early years of my youth."

Doctor: "You are stretching my anticipation ever more. Teach me how you were able to achieve such capacities."

Joiner: "Well now; then listen. I am the son of nice parents, raised in Christianity. Early on it was impressed on me that a providence keeps watch over us which hears our prayers when we do not become weary of offering them to it. I believed this doctrine, for it gave me a happy outlook for my entire life. My belief drove me to pray and not to let up until I found a hearing. Through constant practice my disposition expanded, and I found in myself a new life which I had not known previously. To this I surrendered myself by and by completely, and arrived at the point where I seek all my counsels in eternity, whereby I obtain certainty and calm."

Doctor: "And this way of life also opens to you the future?"

Joiner: "My spirit, I feel, has no past and no future, to it everything is present. The coming days and years reflect themselves in its gleam, and when I am worthy of gazing there, then the past and future are apparent to me."

Doctor: "Thank you. I have devoted myself to science in order to alleviate by spiritual powers the sufferings of humanity, and if you want to be of help to me with your high capabilities, then you will be obliging not only me, but all of humanity."

Joiner: "You are expecting too much from me. For this, I know, I am not called, otherwise would not the spirit have advised me to choose the position of a scholar. I should go through life a simple craftsman, serve the spirit in lowliness, and never be blinded by glory and fame. Therefore forgive me when I ask you to break off and to leave me undisturbed to my business."

The doctor was more baffled than edified by this talk. He had expected new and important discoveries, and found a simple bourgeois mind. He had hoped to find an assistant who would instruct him over things which he himself did not understand, and now saw himself mistaken. He went away peevishly with the thought that so long as he had not himself obtained some practical knowledge of the spirit, he would never raise his methods of healing to a universal means.

Hence he also did not yet give up the plan of winning the journeyman joiner over to himself in order to climb with him to the highest point of somnambulism.

After three days he again went in the company of the journeyman smith to the joiner in order with his help to move the latter to devote his inner power to humanity. Only this time too all his arts of persuasion failed on the firm declaration of the joiner that he would never with his heavenly gifts commit profiteering. He reproached his former travel companion for blabbing about the matter despite his injunction and for driving him from the town through his carelessness.

The journeyman smith grieved over this, begged and implored him to forgive him and to be calm. He had not known that the matter was so important, otherwise he would have certainly remained silent. But now he was ashamed, and wanted to give him all the satisfaction he desired.

The joiner offered him his hand and said, "I forgive you, you did not mean evil; only now I must leave. I must not stay in a place any longer where I am exposed to curiosity. That which I possess, which lives in me and rules me, does not want to be judged and dragged down by human tongues. I must go, and already tomorrow you will not see me anymore."

He went to the master, revealed his decision to him, and asked him not to hinder him, because fate was driving him away from there. The master consented, though unhappily, and cursed the doctor and journeyman smith who had driven a diligent worker from his workshop.

The journeyman smith reproached himself bitterly, had no rest anymore in M..., and made the decision to return to his home town in order to establish himself there. But Krz. went to W..., where he was at work for some time, and then, according to the wishes of his parents, made his way home.

He greeted his family with intimate love, and rejoiced in being with them again. Then he drew his purse from his pocket, and there was in it the same sum in hellers and pfennigs which he had taken on his journey. "Dear parents", he said now; "heaven lead me, and everything happened as it previously announced to me!"

Krz.

In love and contentment he continued his trade as a master now, and remained always true to the higher calling which he received from the spirit.

***

Retrospective

We see here the example of a freer spiritual life than magnetism shows us. Here a sort of power is obtained which is subject to the will of the possessor, even if not entirely, at least already in part; whereas with magnetism external actions must prevail in order to bring the human into the inner life. Krz. knew time and minute when he found himself in the spirit; it was not an isolation from his previous state, his memory bore the experiences from the outer life into the inner life, and vice versa, from the inner into the outer. There was no standstill, no seeming death like we see with the magnetised, but rather the clearest awareness and the purest observation of all the impressions of the outer and inner life, and therefore he is for our task a far more instructive example than all the somnambulists, even if they also gaze just as deeply into the spirit world. Freedom is the human's highest ideal! Free thinking and deciding is laid in him by that eternal power of creation which itself decides and acts in unalterable freedom and unmistakeable truth. Indeed the example put forward still lacks much of that sublime dignity which the inner life is given as enduring and the outer life as passing. But we see in it already a stage reached which places humanity at a standpoint where it speaks not only in empty wordplay about immortality, but rather where the innermost marrow of life develops and offers the possessor the infallible crown of an eternal existence.

Spirit world and immortality condition one another; without spirit world no immortality is thinkable, but this is necessary if the human should pass over to the spirit world.

Immortality is a life power which the can feel, but not analyse. Nobody is capable of explaining why and how you see and hear. The powers of sight and hearing lie in nature, and make themselves known in the creatures. The creature can pass into dust, but those powers cannot.

These views though, I hope, should become far clearer if we bring out several more examples from history which document in all the nuances of life their inner effectiveness, and portray the connection with the spirit world as necessary condition, as the highest requirement for the destiny of the human.

***

Glances into the 17th Century

In the times where metaphysical disputations belonged to everyday history, where parties formed and persecuted each other with bitter hate, the son of a rich merchant had completed his studies, obtained the doctor's cap, and had already lived several years at the university as an adjunct professor, where he surpassed all others through magnificent lectures, and collected audiences from all castes and classes around himself.

L...h, as we want to call him, had affiliated to a party which sought in the finest dialectic and its consequences the epitome of all morals. He went so far that he claimed the life of the human consisted in this art, it was his spirit and his highest destiny.

The agility of his expressions, his acumen, his manners, even in part his splendid figure created for him a fame so that he felt tempted to believe he was called to become a second reformer. Indeed for public life, that he saw well, his doctrine could not be of any use, only in the universities he hoped to work a reformation which would open a new, bolder and more infallible course to scholarship.

So it happened that he one day in giddiness claimed his infallibility: only someone who honoured his doctrine could achieve the true dignity of the human; everything else is subordinate, given, and imposed by dreamers and imitators, without content and seasoning.

A man of mature age who found himself in the lecture hall was astonished at the fire and the boldness of this talk, but could not in the end hold back his judgement anymore and said aloud, "I feel sorry for the speaker that he sold his talent for a fantasy and does not prefer devoting himself to the truth."

This remark made a mighty impression on L...h. Nobody had yet dared contradict him, from fear of his following and the sting of his talk. He lost the thread of his lecture and saw himself forced to leave the lectern. He walked home full of inner rage. "Who is it", he thought to himself; "who abuses me before everyone? Who gives him the right to damn my doctrine? Who is it? I must get to know him, hear him face to face; then I will see whether he withstands my reasons."

He made every effort to learn the name of the stranger and to track him down. For a long time he endeavoured in vain; finally one of his family informed him that he had seen and heard the man again — he was an estate owner, six hours from there, was called Herdtmann, and the place of his residence was R—. L...h had immediately resolved to travel there; he wanted to get to know his enemy, and to assert his system against him at any price.

He arrived at the location. With impatience he waited for the moment to meet the man who threatened to destroy the fruits of his knowledge and his striving. Barely having arrived at the inn, he sent a messenger to the estate owner and had him ask to the gift a stranger an undisturbed discussion.

Herdtmann asked whether the stranger was expecting him in the inn, or wanted to proceed to his house.

Since the messenger could not give an answer, Herdtmann made his way to greet the stranger in the inn.

L...h saw him coming and had the landlord give him a room where he could speak undisturbed with his opponent.

***

New Acquaintance

Herdtmann entered the room and was taken aback a bit when he saw the bold lecturer; but he soon composed himself and thought, who knows whether it will not lead to something good.

L...h greeted him with polite decorum and apologised on account of his insistency. "Only" he added; "I cannot let myself rest over a rebuke which you made me a few days ago in an assembly of numerous people, without drawing the appearance of faintheartedness and of neglect on myself."

Herdtmann looked him sharply in the eye and said, "My good sir! You are right. I had allowed myself an utterance which, even if not unjust, was though affronting. Hence I turn to your magnanimity and ask for forgiveness. A close relative of mine, one of your most zealous adherents, who had already been praising for a long time your doctrine and lectures, talked me into visiting the lecture hall with him in order to convince myself over his judgement. The fire of your talk seized me, the ease with which you solved the most difficult tasks and connected the most distant concepts made me afraid for my relative, and my utterance, which I certainly expressed too loud in a sort of eagerness, applied to him."

L...h: "My good sir, you mention the affront. — It is true you allowed yourself to make suspect my views before a large gathering. I would have to deny my feelings if I wanted to say that it had not wounded me. But more than the affront, I was provoked by your opposition which applied to a matter over which I have thought for years, which I found amongst the hyperbole and principles of the day alone to be truthful and tenable. Before we thus speak about the affront, I call upon you to prove your opposition, or to declare publicly that you did me wrong and your judgement was just as rash as it was thoughtless."

Herdtmann: "You place more weight on the matter than on the affronting way with which I opposed you. It wearies me, for in the second case I was ready to give you any satisfaction that you desired. Indeed, I declare that I was resolved to seek you out in order to even things out, if you had not come to me first. But with regard to the matter itself, there I cannot take back my judgement; it is the truth, and about this I will, if it must be so, wager my life."

L...h: "What, you hope to battle with success against a doctrine which is contained in the nature of the human and is prescribed by it? What higher thing is there than reason, which, when it is ordered and has exhausted all forms of thought, reflects as a mirror the purest truth, and in which everything is cleared up and puts us in agreement with eternity."

Herdtmann: "I see that you are clearing a great field for your matter, and that a struggle with you will not be an easy game; regardless of that I accept the challenge. But, such a dispute is not decided so soon and the inn is not the place for it either; hence I suggest to you that you come to my house and stay there for as long as until everything has been discussed to the last point and decided."

L...h accepted the suggestion and quartered himself at his opponent's place, where he was given a room whose prospect dominated the entire district and involuntarily surprised the guest.

"Consider yourself at home here", Herdtmann said; "for our dispute time will still be found. Only when we have gotten to know each other better will our views be able to be compared with full clarity. Now feel welcome under my roof and give me the pleasure of letting yourself enjoy a few days with me."

L...h could not resist the obliging behaviour of Herdtmann, and promised to make use of his offer.

"Allow me", Herdtmann continued; "to leave you alone for a little while. Business is calling me. There are books here to enjoy, you can also visit my garden and have a look at the area. After eating we will travel together to the tenant farm;

there we will then begin undisturbed our feud which, as I hope, will end without mutual satisfaction."

L...h's feelings had indeed lost the greatest part of its bitterness, but he could not yet accustom himself to the tone of the estate owner. He looked at the small library which was in the room. There were travel descriptions, philosophical and theosophical views; an outline of the universe according to the Ptolemaic system, alongside a comparison of it with the principles of Copernicus. He leafed through the various books for a few minutes, then went to make his way into the garden, but at the same moment Herdtmann entered the room.

"Here I am again", he said; "the business for today is sorted out, now I am entirely at your disposal. The morning is so beautiful! We will go into the garden, and drink there a glass of wine for refreshment and to good acquaintance."

The garden was laid out with taste, but just as much for use. To begin with the wandered silently up and down an alley of fruit trees. A servant brought wine and baking. They sat, drank a little, only the conversation did not want to get going yet. They stood up again, struck out on another path at whose end a large pear tree and an even larger apple tree stood as majestically as if they were the guardians of the garden.

L...h: "Those are two beautiful trees."

Herdtmann: "Certainly; indeed already old, but still prolific."

L...h: "A pear tree and an apple tree?"

Herdtmann: "Yes, and of quite a good sort."

L...h: "Their branches are interwoven as if they are rejoicing at standing by one another."

Herdtmann: "I think they are rejoicing in it, and I find uplift and instruction in the thought that everything in nature strives to unite."

L...h: "Everything strives for union, only the human does not."

Herdtmann: "You cannot say that in earnest. Even humans seek to unite; certainly the threads which draw us to one another are often hidden from us."

L...h: "The must be so, for I do not yet see the magnetic power which could, as it seems, unite our opposed views."

Herdtmann: "All oppositions are already powers of uniting through one cancelling out the other."

L...h: "That is not clear to me."

Herdtmann: "There are no entirely opposed things in nature, otherwise there would have to be a 'nothing' and this is unthinkable. Nothing and something would be entirely opposed to one another; all other things are already closer, and if the diversity at first glance is yet so great, on closer investigation an eternal striving for union is to be found until finally all contradictions resolve themselves."

L...h: "Of these two trees, the one cannot bear any pears, other cannot bear any apples."

Herdtmann: "But both fruits serve us for nourishment."

L...h: "The pear can never become an apple and the apple never a pear."

Herdtmann: "Is this then necessary, since they unite in their end use?"

L...h: "But if the fruit of a tree would be so distasteful that you could not enjoy it at all?"

Herdtmann: "Then it would promote human welfare in another way, and thereby combine with the better one to a goal."

L...h: "And you believe this trait of uniting in a highest goal is present in all beings?"

Herdtmann: "Quite certainly."

L...h: "Even with humans?"

Herdtmann: "Even with them."

L...h: "How can virtues and vices lead to *one* end goal?"

Herdtmann: "It certainly seems strange, and yet it must also be so if the laws of nature do not lie. Virtues and vices. — Light and darkness. — There is no darkness in which light, even if yet so divided, would not be contained. An entirely pure light is to be thought of just as little, because such a thing would abolish the concept of "something" as it were. I am sticking to my claim: all humans have one and the same end goal. Certainly there much may depend on the path which you take up; one person goes straight, another here and there. The one wanders through swamps, the other on drenched meadowland. Our end goal is knowledge of God. Anyone who seeks here the right source can easily arrive at it, but someone who goes astray and contents himself with shimmering hypotheses is distancing himself from the goal, and must atone for it in that he will arrive where he must finally get to, and even if it should only happen after billions of centuries.

I do not know whether I am expressing myself clearly enough," Herdtmann continued; "but the matter is so subtle that it evaporates in the words before it forms itself into a concept. It is also elevated above all concepts, for it belongs to no species and to no race; it is single, alone, existing for itself, eternal and indivisible."

L...h had listened to these words with great attentiveness and replied, "You speak logically, and I cannot set anything against your conclusions. But you do not seem to have touched the main matter. You are silent about the virtues, and leave it to each to investigate themselves whether and what they are. — If we were clear about the concept of them, then no objections would arise. But since each seeks them on his special path and thinks to find them there, new mistakes are always occurring. I therefore ask, what is virtue?"

Herdtmann: "The last goal which the human should reach gives us the doctrine. When we obtain what we are called to, then we are living virtuously; when we distance ourselves from the goal, then we are sinning. Virtue is therefore acting true to the laws of human nature in order to reach the last goal of our existence."

L...h: "Good! What according to your views are the surest means to the goal?"

Herdtmann: "The striving for the knowledge of the spirit."

L...h: "That means development of the understanding and reason."

Herdtmann: "Do these lead to the goal?"

L...h: "They lead to it and are themselves the goal; for in the clearest knowledge the human achieves the destiny of his existence."

Herdtmann: "To which branches of knowledge do you give the preference in this respect?"

L...h: "Arithmetic, mathematics, and the pure, logical dialectic."

Herdtmann: "Accordingly the logician, the mathematician, and the dialectician do not need any religion anymore?"

L...h: "In certain respects, no. Since religion itself is a result of the purest knowledge, it connects with our concepts and appears thereby still in a more perfect light than if we devote ourselves with blind faith to it."

Herdtmann: "I know enough. It is time to eat. After the meal more on this. I know your views now and hope that they will not remain in opposition to mine for all too long."

They went back into the house. A happy family gathered at the table and gave L...h's disposition unnoticed a different mood than he had arrived with.

After the meal a carriage was harnessed. They drove to the tenant farm in order to enjoy the beautiful nature there and to fight out their dispute.

Arriving there they sat down in a secluded arbour and gave instructions that nobody was to be allowed to disturb them. Herdtmann took up the conversation and said, "We are alone, now we want to exchange our ideas with each other and see what fruits emerge from that. But beforehand allow me to share with you a small story from my life."

***

I was at the University of H...r and was considered to be an open-mind, but also a wild thing. The lecturers admired my talents, but were not content with my industry. At merry banquets, however, I mostly received the place of honour because my purse was constantly filled, because I was a good fencer, and knew no fear, even when the greatest superiority stood opposite me. With this way of life it was naturally not without arguments and fights, whereby I was lucky though to always come away from them uninjured. Through that my audacity rose still higher and almost nobody dared anymore to give me a wrong look. One day I went out the town gates with two comrades. Unfamiliar officers encountered us, who, as it appeared, allowed themselves to make remarks about us. — Already I wanted to make them explain themselves, but my companion hindered it. Three days later I noticed those officers in a house in which, according to the talk of the lads, the idol of my life resided, that is, I was mortally in love with the daughter of an official whom the officers were visiting.

New Acquaintance

Already irritable beforehand, I did not hear any reproach from my reason anymore; jealousy with its furies' fire seized me and I was resolved to take revenge.

I revealed this intent to my comrades. They had already caught the officers on similar paths and gave my decision their full applause. It was only about what sort of thing was to be carried out.

If something evil should happen, the opportunity soon presents itself. In the evening we met the officers in a public garden just outside the town. We sought to provoke them, they us, and thus the cause was there for the dispute. Indeed people stepped in-between, which prevented the fight this time. But the matter was not over with that; for insults were exchanged without count and the officers believed they were obliged to the honour of their class to demand satisfaction. But so as to not go to work boyishly, they challenged us to pistols, in order, as per their expression, to drive away the wilfulness of the immature heroes with the view of a certain death.

Our decision was quick. The challenge was accepted, and place, day, and hour appointed. We prepared ourselves in the handling of pistols and in the ordering of our affairs for all possible cases.

The last day before the duel was tending to an end. I had just been occupied in writing to my parents in order to inform them of the necessity of my way of handling things, and to reveal to them my final wishes in case I was killed or required to flee; then my mother, who resided forty hours distance from me, entered my room. I started as if a spirit had approached me from out of the grave. "Mother! Mother!", I cried out; "What do you want here? Now — when I was — expecting you least of all!"

She was in great emotion and said, "You did not suspect my arrival, I believe; only I am here to rescue you from a danger which I do not know, but which threatens you with your downfall. Quick, pack your things together and follow me before it becomes too late."

Paralysed I looked at her and replied, "I cannot follow you, my honour stands at play; this I must not allow to be denounced, and even if it costs me my life."

She became more and more insistent, seized my hand tightly and said, "You must follow me, as true as I am your mother, so true is it that a God is in heaven who wants you rescued by me!! Come, do not lose a moment, or I will make a racket and call the authorities for help!"

"Mother!", I begged; "I cannot; I truly cannot!"

Her: "Only for one day."

Me: "Impossible! Mother, you will plunge me into ruin!"

Her: "No. You are running towards your own ruin if you remain. You must follow me without hesitation or become an evildoer in my eyes."

Without knowing how it happened to me, I gathered together a few things, went with her down the steps, out the door of the house, and saw there her carriage harnessed with post horses. She pulled me in almost violently, gave the post boy a sign, and he drove out like an arrow to the gates.

"Where are you wanting to take me?", I now asked.

Her: "To where I know you are safe; to your parent's house."

Me: "But my lecturers ... the rector ... my comrades ... my honour ... the shame ..."

Her: "I have looked after everything. You have eight days holiday in order to travel to your family for urgent family matters."

I was as though numbed, wanted a few times violently to leap out the coach door, but she did not let go for a moment with her arm which was firmly slung around me, so that it was impossible for me to leave the carriage without putting her in danger.

We drove the whole night through. She had made her arrangements so well that everything was ordered in advance and we were constantly served with fresh horses as quickly as if it were about outrunning death.

After we had driven four stations without pause and the morning sun was already standing in the sky, she said, "Now I feel easy. Son, I have the suspicion you are saved; I had no rest anymore at home, deathly fear drove me up the wall until I had made the decision to fetch you. I saw you in my dreams stained with blood; one time you lay dead before me with a horrible wound, and when I did not pay attention to it, this terrible image followed me even when awake. Praise God! Now you are saved; now tell me what a fate threatened you."

I was barely in a state to bear this tale. My heart was trembling as if it wanted to explode. Now for the first time I recognised the horrible situation in which I found myself. "Death or murder!" These two ideas seized me. "Mother! Mother!", I called after a long internal battle; "You have pulled me back from an abyss in which, as it also would have come to, I would not have found a way out anymore."

Now I told her what happened, and felt with it for the first time the worth of honest sympathy and love; for she, without complaint, without reproach, rejoiced only in the saved son, and pressed me, while a stream of tears surged from her eyes, to her heart as if she had given birth to me for a second time.

After the first outpourings of heart, she said, "Now I must collect myself, begrudge myself some strengthening." At the next post we climbed out, took something to eat, and then drove in a more leisurely way home.

The first thing was now to get news from the university. In a few days the tidings came — the duel had taken place and indeed with pistols at ten paces; a student and an officer had remained at the place, the others had fled over the border.

Only now did the blindfold fall entirely from my eyes. Here in the circle of my parents and siblings, I could imagine vividly what a horror would have come over them if I had taken part in that bloody scene. The impression which these considerations made on me was so great that I made the decision to abandon my wild ways and to give myself over solely to the guidance of my parents. "God saved you!", my mother said. "God saved me!", it echoed on my heart. There is a God and a providence! For the first time since my boyhood, I believed in them. Good! I have talents, so say my lecturers; I want to use them to a higher goal, want to follow the trail which providence showed me and reach the goal which it prescribes for the human.

The desire to return to the university had vanished. I asked my father to suggest another career for me. He advised me to dedicate myself to the science of economics in order to serve the state some day in this subject or to administer on my own account an estate. He sent me to this end into a distinguished private institute where I acquired such thorough knowledge that I considered it to be the most expedient to put my learning to use on my own land, and through advantageous arrangements be of use to the state and my fellow citizens as an example. Thus I have been living here for twenty years, and believe to have fulfilled in every respect that which I gave my word to do.

As I obtained more independence and my character consolidated itself, I returned again and again to the story of the duel. "God saved me!", it still resounded in my heart. "How is it possible", I often asked myself; "that this eternal power looks after the human so wonderfully? How can you learn to recognise it? On what paths should you investigate in order to get closer to it and to notice the driving force with which it touches the human so intimately?" To begin with these were only declarations, arising in effusive hours; but by and by the thought became ever more powerful, turned into a life feeling, and I saw clearly that the happiness of my existence would depend on the knowledge of this invisible influence.

Now my life received a different direction; I read books which I had previously not heeded, sought acquaintances whom I had previously considered superfluous, to become informed about my self-set task was now the single wish of my heart. The Bible, that divine book, which seemed to me to begin with like a collection of folk tales, became more important to me, and I could in the end not help establishing the claim that if God formerly spoke with humans, then he must still do, otherwise he would not be almighty, not infinite, not eternal wisdom and love.

On this I built the plan of my investigations, but where to discover the key to it? As often as I set this question, I could not find the answer, neither with others, nor in books. "Where is the key?", I sighed; "I must obtain it, for without it I possess with all my knowledge nothing. To know that God has an effect is easy, is a matter of blind faith; a child can have it, and is thereby richer than the most learned doubter. I know something, but not the main thing; I believe that there is a God, but cannot approach him, and hence I seem like someone who knows that there is a wealth, but himself has none in his possession."

My yearning for revelation became ever greater and I considered it in the end to be impossible that the Bible could show us such results without at the same time also containing the means which lead us to them. I devoted myself entirely to this consideration and hoped to obtain satisfaction in the New Testament. Verses like these: "Whoever sins against the father, he is forgiven; whoever sins against the son, he is forgiven; whoever sins against the spirit, he can never be forgiven."* Furthermore: "When you pray, do not use lots of words, the heathens do that; when you pray, you should speak thus: Our Father, etc."† now occurred to me for the first time. I considered it to be accepted that here a sense lay hidden whose unveiling was capable of bringing me at once to understandings.

"What does that mean?", I asked. "Is the spirit more than father and son? Or is it perhaps for the human like a leader, or as it were given as a possession with which he should put himself in agreement? Why finally not make lots of words? Do not many words point to understanding and higher development of the spirit?"

I became doubtful anew, but returned again and again to such passages: "You should not use lots of words, but rather should speak thus: Our Father, etc." — "Certainly in this everything is contained which is necessary and useful for the human, but he cannot lower himself to a mere machine and repeat that for evermore", I thus thought and lost myself in conjectures.

I stood there like the wanderer in pitch-black night, and could go neither forwards nor backwards. I felt that I was

---

* [Tr.: cf. Matthew 12:31–32: Wherefore I say unto you, All manner of sin and blasphemy shall be forgiven unto men: but the blasphemy against the Holy Ghost shall not be forgiven unto men. / And whosoever speaketh a word against the Son of man, it shall be forgiven him: but whosoever speaketh against the Holy Ghost, it shall not be forgiven him, neither in this world, neither in the world to come.
Mark 3:28–29: Verily I say unto you, All sins shall be forgiven unto the sons of men, and blasphemies wherewith soever they shall blaspheme: / But he that shall blaspheme against the Holy Ghost hath never forgiveness, but is in danger of eternal damnation.]

† [Tr.: cf. Matthew 6:7–9.]

close to the point on whose decipherment all depended, but I was incapable of grasping the key, as close as it also lay to me.

Finally, after years of long struggle I had found what I sought; it became light in me, and since then I have recognised that all knowing which does not come from the eternal and lead back to it again is nothing more than vanity which nourishes our darkness, but contains no sparks of inner life power.

***

After this story a deep silence occurred. L...h stood up from his seat, and walked back and forth a few times, then he said, "Your tale has over many others of the same content the advantage that the man to whom it happened stands opposite me, since they otherwise usually start with the formula 'N... told me, P... said to him, the neighbour of T... saw with his own eyes, etc.' — They place a great value on self-experience! In your situation it can be no different, because it gave your fate a quite different direction, and hence influenced mightily your way of thinking and feeling. Premonitions and dreams exist; who can deny that? But the free thinker must not take up such chance phenomena into his system, because he would otherwise have to renounce all freedom of knowledge."

Herdtmann: "According to that almost all hope of union between us would be cut off. But I am not giving up my matter as lost yet; I build on the sentence: what happens has more worth than what I merely know. My story is fact, your truths have their basis in the world of ideas; let us lay both on the scales and you will see how little weight the latter has against the former. You indeed claim reason encompasses all the spheres of human knowledge! Now I ask you, what does it know of the future? Nothing; it must not and cannot know anything about it; because it recognises only those principles as valid which it drew from the features in agreement after comparing concepts and ideas. Past and present deliver reason the materials for activity; it is scared of the future, like before a sealed vessel of which you do not know whether it contains poison or honey. And yet the human must, if he lays claim to perfection, and wants to put himself in a class with the immortals, embrace all realms, 'past, present, and future', otherwise he has no whole, his existence is not yet grounded, and he cannot give any account which he himself has not perceived with his senses, or received historically from others; of self-activation and own power, excluding the academic working of the material present, there is no trace to be found."

L...h: "If I conclude through comparison of the past and present for the future, is that not a free activity?"

Herdtmann: "I cannot recognise it as such because no time equates completely to another. There have been theosophists and prophets who wanted to predict from history the events of the future, but experience has punished them every time with lies. Infinity is everywhere we turn our eyes. As little as two humans are entirely alike, just as little can one day be the same as another day in its events; and hence the future will become clear just as little to the forms of reasoning of dialectics as the features of a face will be clear to a painter who has never seen it."

L...h: "This view has much going for it, and I am at the moment not in the position to succinctly refute it. I must confess only so much that if you are right, then my previous striving was a playing with soap bubbles in order to captivate children. But I do not give such easy purchase to be overcome. Admittedly you can counter me with: eternity has revealed itself to you visibly in that supernatural powers saved you from a fate which would have plunged you irrevocably into ruin. Such luck has not been granted to me, and hence I must hold myself to that which I possess, namely to my power of intellect which shows itself to me through the ability to obtain knowledge. Each to his own. You practise philosophy practically, I must treat it theoretically because its knowledge basis does not flow towards me from any visible source."

Herdtmann: "You are giving the school, the fundamental learnedness the highest worth. I would have to condemn the most beautiful feature of social life if I did not have high respect for it; only I cannot consider it to be the last goal of life.

Learnedness, to where does it lead? It gives us the means to order our experiences and consider them systematically. Now I ask, from where does it draw this material? Answer:

from temporal things which are today thus and tomorrow something else. Philosophy? Under how many diverse forms has it already appeared, and how often will it yet change its clothes? If it had grasped its last goal, then it would itself be in its forms more durable and independent. But not only in the forms, no, even in its views it changes, and hence you will forgive me if I endeavour to win you to a view which gives your urge for knowledge an enduring foundation and secures it from deception.

Science, you indeed claim, is to you the revelation which flows from eternity and sets in motion the highest powers of the human. I do not contradict you here, but science goes too far, it leaves its natural soil, separates from human nature, and goes without it into eternity. The human is a feeling being who can connect with love and distance with hate. What we do not love, we do not work on, and even if it were the most previous thing. If we do not hate vice, we have no power against its temptation, and see ourselves, before we suspect it, entwined in its nets. The human is at home in his feelings and safe from all storms. Everything which is supposed to rise to a proper plant must germinate and sprout from feelings. All knowing which estranges itself from feelings is superfluous and even an evil because it robs the tree of its natural driving force and cripples it."

L...h: "I understand you. In the ennoblement of feeling you find the true activity of the human. From feeling, you seem to claim, every piece of knowledge must arise, if it should be beneficial to our high calling in life. I must confess this view is too new for me to be able to get used to it so easily; I also see no possibility for how the free will of the human can exist at the same time; for love and hate, as you say yourself, drive and dominate us. On what lower step would the human stand if it were thus! Still more, love and hate are themselves not free powers, but rather conditioned by external impressions, and hence the human would possess, if we consider him to be a feeling being, not the slightest freedom. In science he places raises himself by his own will, there he places himself at the standpoint where he must decide and choose without urge and passion. Science itself knows no love and no hate, it is only clarity and illuminates those alone who choose it in complete freedom. It places us at the point of an impartiality which grants us the rulership over our activity and itself commands our feelings."

Herdtmann: "These ideas, as shimmering as they are portrayed, have neither continued existence nor result. Anyone can appear and say: my knowing suffices for me, I have no need of the heart. I know well that abstract philosophy imagines the being of God in such independence; but precisely this is the most horrible doctrine. God without love! I do not like to and cannot think it. God with love which devotes itself to the loving creation! From this thought arises the elevating feeling which itself rises to consciousness, and binds heart and knowledge to an end goal. I do not want to talk further, you yourself agree with me, your heart must reaffirm that a complete lovelessness in the kingdom of God and of nature would be more dreadful than death and destruction, and that the most obdurate sinner is not in a position to grasp these thoughts."

L...h felt the weakness he had presented and became embarrassed. Herdtmann noticed it and made the suggestion that they view the beauties of the district a little. They left the arbour, visited a few remarkable points, and drove back home again.

The next morning L...h took his leave of Herdtmann while he said, "Your words have put me in an inner conflict with myself, I must collect myself and compare what I have heard with my own ideas. Many thanks to you for your kind hospitality and please allow me permission to visit you again soon."

Herdtmann offered him his hand and replied, "I have been yearning for a long time already for a man who resists the flittering joys in exchange for the truth, and who lives his higher calling. Believe me, I have discovered many a thing which is foreign to the deepest learnedness, and when you learn to see that the finest speculations subside into a chaos, then I will dare to offer you a key which opens for you the entrance to knowledge which only the perfected man is in a position to obtain and grasp. Farewell! Visit me as often as your inner-being drives you to, and expect that the arms of a friend will embrace you."

Johann Baptist Krebs

L...h drove back to the town and Herdtmann prayed in himself to lead this new acquaintance to the proper goal.

***

L...h's Doubt

L...h arrived home in a strange mood; he had gone to R— in order to make a forward critic explain himself, and returned as his friend. — His resolve to throw away nothing from the system which he himself had drafted indeed stood firm, only he could not find sufficient grounds anymore which he would be able to set against the oracular expressions of Herdtmann in the future. "He seeks the truth", he thought, "and finds it in the belief which was forced on him by a visible event; he speaks of secrets which he wants to unveil to the bold investigator of his time. Only from where will those flow? From the feeling of his belief? It is clear to me, and I will make my preparations before I visit him again."

The next day he collected his friends about him, as usual, to give new information about the dignity of the human and his capability for knowledge. But, without wanting to, sometimes a view of belief merged into his talk, which gave his lecture a touch of hyperbole which you would not have noticed in it previously. Everybody noticed this change, but irregardless of it they were so enraptured by the stream of his eloquence and the new images, which were welling up from his soul unnoticed by him, that he celebrated a double triumph, as man of feeling and as speculative philosopher, at the same time.

The gathering parted; he arrived quietly at his residence. "I am captured", he said to himself; "my talk was warmed by an alien fire, as much as I endeavoured to light it myself. The hyperbole has its own power; it conquers the heart, creeps from this to the brain, and is through that ruler of our thoughts. How weak the human is though when he has no base of support in his most important realisations, when he must be dominated by feelings which are not his own and which are breathed into him by others as it were. I must pull myself together, otherwise, I clearly see, I will lose myself in a labyrinth from which I will not find the way out. Me or him! One must be right. In the last goal the truth cannot be twofold, it can only be one thing — thus me or him; one of us must be the victor!"

For three days he held out in his struggle; on the fourth he drove to Herdtmann in order, as he said, to be the victor or be defeated.

***

Second Visit

Herdtmann received him amiably, and showed him again to the same room to reside in. "It delights me", he said; "that you so soon kept your word to visit me. I have these days often thought of you, and if I may trust my intuition, then the honest wish to get clear over things which seem puzzling to you is what leads you to me."

L...h: "So it is. This time I am here in order to unload all the doubt which our last discussion brought forth in me. You or me; only one can be right, of that I am perfectly certain; hence allow me a question. Can you give me information about the last goal of the human?"

Herdtmann: "Yes."

L...h: "And what is this goal?"

Herdtmann: "To find himself in the whole as an individual who lives in accordance with his destiny."

L...h: "What is the whole?"

Herdtmann: "Everything."

L...h: "Through what does everything distinguish itself from the whole?"

Herdtmann: "Through its epitome."

L...h: "I do not understand that."

Herdtmann: "I believe it. You must wait until the point in time comes."

L...h: "You are speaking new puzzles."

Herdtmann: "Not entirely, for it will become clear."

L...h: "When?"

Herdtmann: "When the spirit is victorious."

L...h: "What difference is there between thought and spirit*?"

Herdtmann: "Thought emerges from the spirit. It is the child of it and gives back to it again what it receives from outside."

L...h: "That sounds good, but I cannot grasp the sense."

Herdtmann: "Thought comes from the spirit, the spirit of the human flows from the whole, the whole is spirit in which everything is contained. Do you understand me?"

L...h: "Not entirely."

Herdtmann: "When the one reveals itself, the other also becomes clear. When the individual is recognised, only then do we recognise the whole."

L...h: "How is the individual to be recognised?"

Herdtmann: "Through the thought if it is practised."

L...h: "How do you practise it?"

Herdtmann: "You let it come to you of itself so that it can itself move in itself. You do not bind it with vain tethers, so that its wings stir by themselves. We must serve it, not it us; for it is the master which can ruin us or lead us to life."

L...h: "I am astonished. These sentences are as simple as the easiest tasks of arithmetic; but they flow past my ears and do not want to set root in me. Why not?"

Herdtmann: "You are not feeling them and want merely to know, hence the content flies by so quick that you barely notice the traces of it. But it will change when we are more closely acquainted. Now let us be in good spirits and happily celebrate the present day."

In the afternoon they went about the neighbourhood in order to see a few curiosities. Their conversations were insignificant and referred to the news of the day in a political and scientific respect.

The next morning when Herdtmann came to his guest's room and asked him how he had slept, the latter answered, "Good, with the exception of a few rapturous dreams which set my blood churning. I saw myself as a soldier for a matter which was yet unknown to me, and when I desired

---

* [Tr.: note that the German word for spirit [*Geist*] can also mean intellect, mind, or ghost. Spirit has been mainly used as the translation throughout here.]

Second Visit

information, I received only the answer that the struggle is given to you; only from this does the true knowing sprout. You see, I come towards you at least in dream, but waking I remain still with my maxim, you or me! Only one can be right.

Yesterday you placed both our views opposite one another in order to examine them more surely. I want to do it now too, and think it will lead to a different result.

Your doctrine arises from eternity; it is of supernatural nature. From this you deduce the visible creation and the human. An event of your earlier years serves you as a foundation on which you are building the system of your knowledge. Now I would like to surely ask whether it would then not be possible that that event could have happened in the usual way? Would it then be entirely unthinkable that your mother at the time had received news which made her afraid? Now you well know, if the heart is stirred up once, it plays on and creates dreams, presentiments, indeed even apparitions. Enough, I cannot build on such grounds. I consider a matter as it is, compare it with others, judge its features, draw conclusions from them, and have thereby performed an act of the spirit. You stand on invisible territory, I stand on firm ground. You are deducing from the invisible the visible, and I the reverse. The invisible, however, is not to be tested, therefore the conclusions which you draw from it are uncertain and cannot hold water before the judgement seat of reason."

Herdtmann: "To whom is science suited?"

L...h: "To the human."

Herdtmann: "To all?"

L...h: "Mainly to scholars or those who understand their language."

Herdtmann: "To whom belongs belief?"

L...h: "To all humans."

Herdtmann: "Well now; so it already has an advantage over science."

L...h: "Belief and science are two regions; where science stops, the other begins."

Herdtmann: "Is there belief without science?"

L...h: "That does not seem surely possible."

Herdtmann: "What must the devout one know?"

L...h: "He must recognise in himself that there is a God."

Herdtmann: "This is yet no science."

L...h: "Oh yes. Anyone who recognises his feelings knows and steps thereby into the region of science."

Herdtmann: "Is self-knowledge of the feelings necessary for belief?"

L...h: "Yes."

Herdtmann: "Is it not enough if he supports himself on others, if he follows authorities, subordinates his feelings and cognitive abilities to them, and merely believes?"

L...h: "It is also enough if it satisfies him."

Herdtmann: "A visible goal, satisfaction, you grant finally to belief?"

L...h: "Belief is mainly a matter of feeling, and must therefore have an effect on our external state of life."

Herdtmann: "Where does true belief have its roots?"

L...h: "In the human himself."

Herdtmann: "Who placed it in him?"

L...h: "Nature."

Herdtmann: "Who placed it in nature?"

L...h: "One moment. — I must think things over. Is nature and God not one thing?"

Herdtmann: "Not entirely. How did you arrive at that question?"

L...h: "Because I am uncertain and am going astray there in spheres where I do not see a way back anymore."

Herdtmann: "You have evaded me. You want absolutely to rescue for the human his mastery; but you have, while we speak, already given up a few times."

L...h: "That I would not know."

Herdtmann: "You cannot believe without knowing. Well now, I ask once more, what must the devout one know? For that he is still required to believe in something other than in himself arises from the matter itself."

L...h: "He must know that is capable of believing."

Herdtmann: "Is this capability necessary for him?"

L...h: "Yes."

Herdtmann: "Why?"

L...h: "In order to find reassurance for the last goal of his life."

Herdtmann: "Is this capability given to all humans?"

L...h: "Certainly."

Herdtmann: "If someone did not have it?"

L...h: "They would be ... You have surprised me with this question."

Herdtmann: "Well, what would he be?"

L...h: "Poor. A lost creature."

Herdtmann: "Accordingly belief would be a necessity for the human?"

L...h: "So it seems."

Herdtmann: "Do you not believe it?"

L...h: "I must believe it, if I do not want to take from the human a base of support which holds together rich and poor, great and small, learned and ignorant, and leads them to one goal."

Herdtmann: "You have expressed what I would not have trusted myself to say. Belief is a necessity in the nature of the human which like hunger and thirst seeks satisfaction. Anyone who is carrying it still pure and unadulterated in themselves must not be told what he should believe; he is required to, like the hungry and the thirsty who know of themselves what they need. Have you yet anything to object to that?"

L...h: "No. I expressed it myself. The conclusions are correct. I vacate the field for you on this point and believe, like you, in the necessity of belief."

Herdtmann: "It is enough. Truly, I would like to thank you for your self-denial which allowed you to pay homage to the truth even against your intention. In this moment we have moved a good step closer to each other, and if you continue with such impartiality, then you will obtain for your science a ground which, the more you cultivate it, the more splendid the fruits it bears. Enough for today. Let us walk in the open air in order to give our feelings a freer room to move."

They visited the garden. Herdtmann spoke to his people about their work. L...h took part by and by in everything, and felt for the first time what a beneficial impression free nature made on the human.

Herdtmann noticed this mood and said, "You have sought up to now your knowledge of humanity in books and at the lectern, but did not think that only in nature can the human find himself. Self-knowledge was with you a degree of knowing, but you forgot that only the free power which germinates naturally grows and produces fruits, and arrives at its perfection. Standstill and calm are necessary for the human if his characteristics should develop, just as in the plant kingdom no tree and no bush can develop properly if it is lacking standstill and calm. The driving force lies in nature; the more undisturbed this works, the more powerful are its creations."

The day passed amidst such conversations. The next morning L...h returned to the town. His students, from whom he had since withdrawn for some days, urged him to continue his lectures and talks punctually. He was embarrassed, for he did not know how he should continue on without showing the perceptible weaknesses of his system. But he let himself be convinced to take the lectern again the next day. His decision spread with lightning speed through the town, and when the hour struck, the lecture hall was packed full.

L...h had had an uneasy night. His victory was already doubtful to him. Now he was supposed to speak as a lecturer to a large gathering who, familiar with his system, were waiting for more reinforcement of the same. He stepped uncertainly into the hall, looked timidly at the crowd and instead of delighting like formerly, he climbed with a feeling of fear to the lectern. He began his lecture without being conscious of the theme, and ended up, as it were as if driven by an inner presentiment, on the changeability of the human, with which the human today embraces this, tomorrow that; recognises in this hour as infallible what he already in the next swaps with a different view. Now he was drawn into the investigation of to what extent this characteristic lead to good versus evil. "Changeability", he said; "is weakness, but on the other hand stubbornness is no virtue. There is also here a middle way which leads to the truth." In this sense he continued speaking so instructively and convincingly that everyone shouted the most unfeigned thanks to him and begged him to soon delight them again with such a lecture.

Second Visit

L...h withdrew quietly. His students wanted indeed to accompany him, but he forbade it. Arriving home, he walked slowly up and down the room musing. "It cannot be thus," he said finally to himself. "This or that, I must pursue one thing. I cannot be Herdtmann's student and teacher of my own system at the same time. — How shall I free myself from this struggle?"

He had no more rest anymore and driven as it were by inner longing, he hurried to the gates and the open air. "How dear nature has become to me!", he cried out when he saw the beautiful landscape lying before himself in the soft sunlight. "Here wafts Herdtmann's spirit which leads us to believing. Here is uninterrupted activity, without force and without given rule. The eternal law of nature creates and works without worrying about the tinkling of human ideas. What shall become of me?!", he sighed. "Should I throw myself entirely into the arms of my new friend and abandon my students, or draw back from a doctrine which I do not know yet, and which in the end will perhaps also not deliver any certain results?"

Almost an hour's walk had distanced L...h from the town and the ever lower setting sun forced him to turn around. He entered the town with a certain apprehension. He looked at the beautiful houses, the glorious towers, and thought, "That is the work of man, but nevertheless great! Outside is nature, no less beautiful and in eternal activity. From these buildings a past power speaks to me, but the works are dead. Outside the powers are eternally young, and hence there new life is always glowing. To what side should I turn? Where will I now find advice which is infallible and correct? I cannot linger any longer, tomorrow I must visit my friend."

***

Third Visit

"Here I am again already!", he called out to Herdtmann as he entered his room. "The town does not want to tolerate me anymore, and where else shall I seek my refuge than with you? Now I am here to entrust myself entirely to your guidance or to part from you forever. You have brought about a split in my soul which is robbing me of the freedom to think and to act. Let me one more time examine your doctrine so that I can convince myself as to whether it will suffice for me or whether I should dedicate my entire life to dialectic."

Herdtmann: "You have passed judgement yourself. Dialectic, and were it yet so pure to dedicate one's life to, remains a task which is not to be solved. The youth can delight in it because they adorn it with flowers; for the old it becomes a mummy which leaves behind for them nothing but an empty skeleton. Look around in the history of the present and past for whether you can find a single one for whom it sufficed right to the grave. Thus away with it, so long as you just listen to yourself! But if you give material to it from another realm, if you enrich it with eternal laws, then you are building altars before which future races will yet recognise the truth and pay homage to it."

L...h: "You may be right. Yes, I feel that this alone is the standpoint on which learnedness reaches its true goal. Teach me how I should begin in order to avoid any detours; lead me so that I do not stumble when supposed mistakes occur to me, and show me the track on which truth and deception are to be properly distinguished."

Herdtmann: "It is! I want to try, whether I succeed, to open your heart so that a higher knowledge illuminates you. But I must go to work slowly and carefully; for it is difficult to climb from the multiplicity in which you have enthused up to now down to the simplicity which my doctrine demands."

L...h: "Everything shall happen as you wish; just give me conviction."

Herdtmann: "It is precisely this which germinates and grows slowly because it must rise to the feeling which life belongs to in its entire extent."

L...h: "Just give me one key so that I can try to at least open a portal."

Herdtmann: "You possess it already; you yourself have pointed to it when you recognised believing to be a necessity."

L...h: "I recognise it more and more to be so, but do I also possess the necessity? Can a new system not dissuade me again from my current conviction and offer me a new necessity?"

Herdtmann: "Not so easily as you imagine. The root of belief lies deeper than that of external realisations. We feel its beneficial influence, and the human does not easily give up what makes him happy! Hence courage! Soon you will obtain more precise information."

Herdtmann was called away. A friend from far-off parts whom he had not seen in a long time had come to visit in order to renew the old friendship.

He was a chemist, the like of which there were many at that time, who explained from the essences of the visible material the ladder which nature takes in order to finally bring forth on the highest rung feelings and thoughts. He had heard of Herdtmann's seclusion from the world, of his power of belief, and wanted to deliver to him through his distillations and digerations the proof evidently of which ways belief forms.

Herdtmann received him heartily. When he noticed what direction the development of his spirit had taken, he well saw that he would rob him of many a beautiful hour. But he thought, "Patience is a virtue. Good for me if it is not given any harder test."

He showed him a room near to a separate kitchen so that he would have the opportunity for toiling away and stirring things together.

Third Visit

Herdtmann informed L...h of the arrival of the new guest. "I hope", he said; "his present shall not disturb us. He is a chemist for whom the spirit world is only worth something when he can skilfully manipulate and show it."

L...h: "I know the like. I would have almost once allowed myself to take up the laboratory apron, only the visibility of spirits could not suffice for me and I thereby arrived at the dialectic."

Herdtmann: "You did well in that; for that is a step closer to the truth, because it seeks its essence in the power of comparison, and distances itself thereby from the material."

L...h: "How many steps are there yet to truth?"

Herdtmann: "This question everybody answers according to their individual situation; because they usually consider the point on which they stand to be the highest."

L...h: "Accordingly everybody reaches their goal?"

Herdtmann: "In their opinion admittedly."

L...h: "But they hover in error. Who frees them from it?"

Herdtmann: "Nature in its unchangeable law which has only one goal, eternity."

L...h: "And with this I am again trounced. But you are right, I feel it. What can the human yet desire if he possesses eternity? I want to accustom myself to think of only this one thing so that I obtain a firm standpoint."

Herdtmann sought to strengthen him in this resolve and went away again in order to make some arrangements. L...h was irked that this accursed chemist had to arrive just then.

"Herdtmann", he thought, "was so beautiful in flight! Now he stands between us two, and both of us will want to be taught by him."

He walked up and down the room amidst such thoughts for a short time, then took himself out into the open air and only returned at lunchtime.

Herdtmann had made the arrangement that he and both his guests would eat alone in order to make them properly acquainted with one another.

The topic of discussion was like it usually is with such company — God, nature, humanity in all respects, learnedness, practical philosophy, and finally also chemistry. According to the stranger's remarks, this was the single art and science which created the single means to knowledge, the unadulterated path to truth on which the human alone recognised the destiny of his existence.

Herdtmann took little part in the conversation.

L...h had already been listening patiently for a long time; but from time to time sought to obtain justice for other branches of knowledge. But the chemist did not allow the validity of any opposition. "All other sciences", he said; "are conditioned again by another, thus not free and independent. Chemistry, however, works as it were with itself, because it makes the uppermost law of thought clear in its essences."

L...h could not hold himself any longer. He now praised for his part dialectics amongst all sciences as the highest, because it stood instructing above all, and gave them names, bounds, indeed even their content. Chemistry he described as a sort of craftwork which existed by mechanical industry and only through this had come to accidental discoveries. "It has no single absolute principle," he remarked; "and has achieved everything only through arduous, craftwork-like experience."

Now the grenade had been thrown. The chemist, full of venom and gall, maintained his views with fire. L...h by contrast abandoned himself entirely to the force of eloquence and drove the chemist thus into the corner so that he finally turned to Herdtmann and declared directly to him that he could not exist under the same roof as such a man. He called dialectics the horror of devastation, the second Sodom and Gomorrah, the eternal Babylon where nobody understood the other and yet everybody thought they possessed the philosopher's stone. — He left the company quite indignantly, packed his things in a great hurry, and left there the next day.

L...h found himself in a painful situation. He was the cause of a breach between two old friends; he had abused his position as a guest because he had driven another guest away through being self-opinionated. He saw this and made efforts to make good his error, but in vain; the chemist did not listen to him, and when he wanted to offer his hand to him as he climbed into the carriage, the latter pushed him away with the assurance that he did not want to have any communion with an enemy of humanity who seduces through cleverly placed words.

Third Visit

Herdtmann watched calmly all these scenes and took no part in them apart from the usual forms of politeness. But L...h barely dared approach his friend after the departure of the chemist. Finally he forced himself and went to him in order to likewise take his leave.

Herdtmann: "What! You want to distance yourself from me too?"

L...h: "I must in order to punish myself for my behaviour."

Herdtmann held him back in that he put to him that it was not good to abandon the young shoot of a plant to itself and expose it to the storms.

L...h: "I understand. Why protect me when you are exposing the other one to the bad weather?"

Herdtmann: "Nothing was to be changed there anymore. He has his fixed goal which he is not to be moved from anymore."

L...h: "But is it the right one too?"

Herdtmann: "For him quite certainly."

L...h: "And my goal?"

Herdtmann: "Is not yet established. Remain here a few days and draw from the incident the teaching that one-sidedness well comprehends a part of the truth in itself, but it can never encompass it entirely."

L...h became thoughtful at this remark and said, "I will remain and want to try to break through the limits which fantasy and egotism have adduced around me."

***

New Acquaintance

One day Herdtmann said, "Up there in the forest, about one hour from here, I have a friend whom we want to visit; you will not rue having made his acquaintance. Wandorf is his name; he was Professor of Mathematics and held that chair with honour; only his science deserted him and without other assistance he would have perished."

L...h became attentive and replied, "You seem to want to attack me from all sides in order to be all the more certain of your victory. Lead me, but make allowances for a newcomer."

They went on their way. A rough path lead upwards to the forest until they arrived at a plateau where a quite large country house stood which the Professor rented. He was sitting in a little garden which lay before the house and gazing calmly in front of himself. But hardly had he perceived the arrivals than he stood up, went towards them, and offered Herdtmann his hand with the question, "What leads you here to me?"

Herdtmann: "I had the desire to see you again in order to learn what whims you are dwelling on."

Professor: "No whims, only realities. Whom do you bring? A relative or someone who out of curiosity wants to admire me?"

Herdtmann: "You should get to know him. Bring us some seats so that we can rest a little."

Professor: "That shall soon be done."

He fetched chairs. After they had sat down in a circle, Herdtmann continued, "I wanted to see whether this isolation is not yet burdensome for you."

Professor: "It becomes more bearable for me from day to day. I am content, live undisturbed for my better self, and do not worry at all about the concerns and plans of the so-called educated world."

Herdtmann: "It is not needed either. But you should give the world an example of how little you need in order to be contented."

Professor: "That I do not dare. I have luckily reached the shore and should not commit myself to the stormy sea again. No, truly, no! That the heroes, the strong spirits may do, I am letting it be. I have indeed found myself with your help, but I do not have your power that I could stroll calmly and with firm steps amongst the deceptions of humanity."

L...h now also took part in the conversation, brought the Professor's attention to the one-sidedness of his way of life, and suggested that it could not possibly be the intention of the creator that humans withdraw themselves from other humans.

Professor: "I know this saying; it seduced me for a long time. But now I believe only in myself and in nature."

L...h: "In yourself?"

Professor: "In who else then? I must be my guarantor for everything if every an accounting is made; no other stands in there for me, and hence I consider it to be my first duty to take care of myself."

L...h: "This doctrine is unfamiliar to me."

Professor: "That can well be, but it is true though. I also lived for a long time in the world; have even acquired fame as a mathematician, for I wrote a book about my science. I considered it to be higher than everything and taught it too in this sense. All at once I became sick, my brain threatened a deadly inflammation; for a long time I could not think and compare anymore. When I had recovered, I wanted to return again to my usual occupation; but there it was found that my nervous system could not endure it and I had to give up mathematics for a long time, if not forever.

Being tossed out of heaven into the abyss may be irksome, but only with this image is my state at the time to be compared. The science which I lived, which I taught, which was my life's goal, and which I shared with others as such, I was supposed to give it up because a few nerves bristled against it and the doctors considered it to thus be good.

New Acquaintance

I lapsed into a sort of torpor where I could not suffer anyone around me. My situation caused a stir, and people who previously had not worried about me now attended to me. So too my friend Herdtmann; he did not satisfy himself, however, with mere news, but rather came to me in my room as a rescuing angel. In the first moment the following conversation unfolded between us:

Him: 'You are ill?'
Me: 'Just recently I was.'
Him: 'Thus it is going better.'
Me: 'No.'
Him: 'Why not?'
Me: 'I have lost myself during the illness.'
Him: 'How did that occur?'
Me: 'I must not practise my favour studies, mathematics, anymore because of nervous weakness.'
Him: 'Then you must grasp something else.'
Me: 'How is that possible. My life, my confidence, in a word my entire self was in my science. With the loss of it I am lost, living dead.'
Him: 'You must choose something which no trouble and no illness can steal from you.'
Me: 'If mathematics could not protect me, where yet is something certain?'
Him: 'In belief.'

With this answer I turned contemptuously from him and did not consider him worthy of an answer. But he remained standing casually before me and said finally, 'You are pushing away the salvation which I offer you?'

Me: 'Such ancient means are not for my condition.'
Him: 'And yet it is the only thing which can help you.'
Me: 'In what dose is it taken?'
Him: 'According to the relationships of the ideas which you have of matters of belief.'
Me: 'Belief is an open field from which anyone can take what they like.'
Him: 'Well! Then choose.'
Me: 'I cannot pass from a positive science to reveries.'
Him: 'You call reveries believing in a whole of which the human is a part?'

Me: 'No, that I call not so.'

Him: 'You call reveries believing in a power in God and nature which gives its abilities to the human?'

Me: 'No, that I also call not so.'

Him: 'Now, so you have already the belief which I suggested to you. Seek out the relationships in which you stands to the whole, then you are safe and your self is found again.'

Here I turned to him again and looked at him, like you look at someone who has the judgement over our life and death in their hands, and shows us hope of reprieve. He said much more, but I had only my relationship to the whole and my self to be regained in mind. I asked him finally to leave me alone and begrudge me time to get used to his ideas and to set them in agreement with my own.

He went away, but came back the next day and asked, 'Now, how is it? Has my medicine exercised its influence already?'

Me: 'I do not know. I am beginning to doubt, and through that I obtain activity again. But one thing strikes me which worries me. If your doctrine of belief is true, then indeed everything which we believe is also present.'

Him: 'Certainly.'

Me: 'So the wondrous stories of India and all the nonsense which gives us the stories of magic are also true.'

Him: 'Who says that?'

Me: 'Your doctrine.'

Him: 'I am saying everything which you can believe of the whole, which agrees with your self, is true.'

Me: 'And this agreement would be the limit which protects us from nonsense and superstition?'

Him: 'Certainly.'

Me: 'And this doctrine?'

Him: 'Is a doctrine of nature. — Your self has gone under because it did not stand in agreement with the whole. The belief which once strikes root cannot go under anymore; to the contrary it grows, it strengthens, and awakes with each morning in renewed and rejuvenated glory. It can never deceive us, never become dangerous to us; indeed, when everything deserts us, even if creation breaks, it is itself enough and carries us through all regions to the eternal power which has been since the beginning and can never stop.'

With these words I was overcome. I sank into the arms of my doctor, like I do now, and thanked him for the saving of my life, my confidence, and my new existence.

My decision was quickly made. I threw all the mathematics books in the fire, moved to the country in order to learn undisturbed to believe, and have through daily practice recognised this art as that which does not numb our brain, does not weaken our health, but rather gives us in all affairs strength and clarity."

Much more was spoken about this subject; finally Herdtmann recalled that it was time to go home. L...h did not like to part from the new acquaintance; his seriousness, mixed with whimsy, had pleased him, and he asked whether it would be unpleasant for him to accommodate a guest for a few days. "That comes down to the guest", he gave in answer. "Good! I'm for it", L...h said; "and if Mr Herdtmann is not offended, I will accompany him to the exit from the forest and return." The Professor was content, Herdtmann likewise, and thus they accompanied the latter halfway home and came back on a different path to the country house again.

The Professor did not worry much about his guest, let him do as he liked, and continued his work and exercises. When the sun was about to set and the shadows of the trees were veiling their residence already in darkness, they sat down again in the garden and discussed this and that. Finally the Professor asked in what way he had come into such close connection with his friend? L...h told him the entire sequence of events up to the current deciding moment.

Professor: "You are of a good path. Continue and you will achieve complete fulfilment."

L...h: "What results can I be accorded?"

Professor: "Clairvoyance, feeling of belief, life in the purest, divine, unchangeable, which brightens the future for us, illuminates the present, and connects us every moment with God and his eternal nature."

L...h: "What are the means to it?"

Professor: "There are many; you have yourself expressed several. The quite simple ones I must not unveil to you, these you must expect from our friend Herdtmann."

During this conversation night had fallen. They went back into the house and soon lay down to sleep.

L...h believed he had been transported to another world. Accustomed from his youth on to residing in towns and splendid guesthouses, this contrast worked forcefully on him and he could not comprehend that there were also no teachers who sought in simplicity the aim of existence. He slept only a little, and barely had the morning dawned than he was already in the garden again.

The forest formed an opening to the east. L...h had indeed already often seen the rising of the sun; but at the time he gave himself the opportunity to speak magnificently over it, now he believed he was seeing an image of God. "Nature is infinitely great!", he cried out enthusiastically. "Who can see it without being astonished, without worshipping."

The Professor stepped out of the house now. "You think", he said; "with me is it beautiful? I sought out this place especially in order to enjoy the spectacle of the sunrise quite often. It becomes day in nature, I think then; in the human it must not remain darkness."

They spoke more about various subjects. The Professor admired the acumen of his new friend who often from one word made a whole hierarchy of conclusions. But the latter found in his new acquaintance an unusual depth of feeling which made clear to him why he separated himself from humans and preferred seclusion. "For", he thought; "an all too great a sensitivity of the heart is not suited to the world because it is injured too often."

L...h remained the entire day and the following night with the Professor. He made every effort to observe his steps, to watch his movements, when Wandorf thought himself alone, in order to arrive on the trail of that mysterious activity over which he still had to expect the information from Herdtmann.

The day passed quickly for him. At sunrise he was again in the garden and filled his heart one more time with the sublime view. When the Professor also appeared and both consumed a small breakfast, L...h gave his leave. The

Professor accompanied him until the edge of the forest and called on him to be steadfast on the life path on which their friend Herdtmann would lead him.

He arrived at Herdtmann's house quite changed. It was as if those two days had poured a new life into him. "What to do now?", he asked when he saw his friend. "I cannot anymore be a lecturer, I feel this, but how can I free myself from the chair without injuring my reputation?"

Herdtmann: "That is easily done if you choose the right means."

L...h: "I find none."

Herdtmann: "Strange. It would all have to have deceived me, or there is found amongst your audience people who have long wished for your removal in order to stand in your place."

L...h: "That I do not believe."

Herdtmann: "It comes down to the attempt. Make it known today and tomorrow your chair is possessed."

L...h blushed at this claim. He had previously considered it to be impossible that someone could replace him, and Herdtmann spoke so confidently of it that he considered him for the first time to be half an enemy of humanity. "Good!", he said; "I want to make the attempt. If someone is found, if this yet comes true, then the world has abandoned me, and I am entirely yours."

He wrote at once to one of his friends, shared his decision with him to not continue teaching, and asked him to make this known so that another could take his place. With heavy heart he held the letter in his hands. The memory of his fame and his activity had an effect on him, and he considered that which he had now done to be a violent break in his life, from which a new would have to germinate if it should not pass away without trace. He finally gave the letter to a servant and then said aloud, "It has happened! A new sun must illuminate me."

He spent two days quite and alone until he received news from the town. Finally a letter arrived. One of his students, G...th by name, had flown into his place and to the admiration of all the audience had held his first lecture. "Herdtmann", he now said to himself; "knows humans better than I do. I have made many a conclusion in my former career and I believe now that I am not wrong in concluding that his knowledge is of a better sort that my own. Hence I want to go to his school." He sought him out in his room, gave him the letter and asked him to now accept him wholly and to lead him to the true goal.

Herdtmann offered him his hand and said, "Welcome to me, into a new dignity. Up to now you have paid homage to your class, now the human must assert itself, and it will be good for you if you succeed in drawing it forth from all the veils."

***

L...h as Student

After four days which L...h spent with varying emotions, he went to Herdtmann and said, "The student comes and asks his teacher to give him instruction in the art of life."

Herdtmann: "You are right; it is time. Every lost day is like a debt which is not to be paid off anymore. So listen: if everything dies, the creator cannot die. — If everything dies, the creation in which the creator is transfigured cannot die either. To seek that, to realise his transfiguration in us, is the task. There are many means, but they take different steps. A few work slowly, others quicker. Anyone who possesses the courage and power can choose the latter. To the weak you must give easy means. Under what class to you count yourself surely?"

L...h: "I possess courage, but whether also power, that I am not sure about. I do not indeed know the actions that I should perform; hence act according to your own judgement."

Herdtmann: "Well! Then listen: have the human in you think, then it is achieved."

L...h: "How?"

Herdtmann: "Have the human in you think, then it is achieved."

L...h: "I suspect I know what you want to say. Pure human nature! Will I ever be able to find it in me?"

Herdtmann grasped his hand, looked him firmly in the eye and said, "Anyone who has courage and persistence, to him no goal is too far." He went into an adjoining room in order to leave L...h to his own judgement.

"Let the human in you think", L...h repeated several times after one another when he saw himself alone. "And I — who am I then?", he asked himself. "Am I not human? Do my earlier realisations not belong to human nature, or are they fruits of strange relationships, false education, and other conventions of the world? And even if so, do they thus remain any less my property? — I arrive anew at confusion. Where do I find pure human nature?"

Here the Professor occurred to him at once. "I know where I will find it!", he called out loud. "There on those forested heights there lives a pure one who has thrown off the veils and stands there in the glow of found human dignity. To him! To him! In his vicinity I will be free of foreign influences."

L...h set off, met Wandorf before the house and revealed to him immediately his doubt. The latter called on him to be persistent and to at least sacrifice a few months to the matter.

L...h listened to him, and rented a house in a village where he could live for his meditations undisturbed. Only after two months did he return to Herdtmann and say, "I have not let the time go by unused; the traces of humanity are becoming clear to me, and I recognise gradually that I possess two selves — one which the world gave me, and another which nature gave me."

Herdtmann looked at him amiably and replied, "When the human in both selves is found, the most difficult step has been taken. Only advance boldly so that I may soon give you more precise information."

L...h had indeed expected to receive it already now, only he took it in his stride and asked, "When may I come again?"

"In two times two months", was the answer.

L...h went back to his village and remained there. Only once, when he almost could not tame his impatience, did he visit the Professor in order to receive strength from him. The latter gave it to him with happy heart and brought his attention to the high goal which was to be reached.

After four months L...h appeared again at Herdtmann's. "The time has passed", he said; "which you specified. I do not know whether I have moved forwards in the meantime; only I now see many things with different eyes; I am calmer, have become more rational, if you will, and am beginning to comprehend that the creation is not there on account of the human, but so that he can cultivate himself in it and ground his existence."

Herdtmann listened full of joy to these words and said, "You have complied fully with my expectations; this obliges me to also comply with my own and to lead you further on the path you have entered. So listen then to what I will now say; but do not interrupt me, for I am saying what I have to and must not get drawn into any explanations.

You obtain knowledge of the spirit when you strive to recognise its characteristics. These characteristics are the component parts of its being. You can possess them theoretically and practically. The theory suffices to name them and to know that they are present. The practice, however, penetrates into their being and into their activity. The latter is our task, and through that we obtain entry into the spirit world.

'You should not use many words", says the Bible. "When you want to pray, you should thus pray: Our Father, etc.'*

With this it is expressed that you should not pray in any other way but this; repeat it so quietly and so often that not only your mouth, but your heart, indeed, your entire nature from the skin to the innermost point of your body learns it by heart. When you then feel the effects of it, when your hair stands on end, when your bones burn, then think: you have received the baptism. Now go or stay with me. In the practice lies the solution. It seems little, but for performing it the highest power of the man is demanded."

He went out and left his astonished student in a whirl of thoughts which set him in the most painful uncertainty. "To learn by heart", he thought, "is that the task of a man for the man? What should I do? — Obey? — Blindly? — For the first time in my life I am commanded to such an obedience which does not allow me even to think. I feel it, I am standing at the crossroads. One way or the other, I must accomplish one thing. But, am I still free? Have I not already surrendered myself? Can I still choose? No! I am bound and must blindly perform the received command."

He walked slowly up and down the garden. Finally he stood still and asked himself, "Should I stay or should I go? Stay? Then I am under his eyes and feel the pressure of the

---

*   [Tr.: cf. Matthew 6:7–9.]

teacher. Go? Then I am somewhat free and even if I am blindly obeying."

He sought out Herdtmann, took his leave of him, and asked, "When may I return again?" — "When the baptism is past", was the answer.

L...h went to his village and began the exercises, not from conviction, but rather in order to make the attempt. For several months he continued them daily for many hours, and returned at the conclusion of five months to Herdtmann and said, "I have the baptism."

Herdtmann examined him and found the statement confirmed. "Remain a short time with me", he said; "until it is fitting to give you the second practical teaching."

On the third day Herdtmann came to him in his room, and had him tell him how and what he had felt and learned. L...h explained each thing especially and Herdtmann then said, "You are called and as I hope also chosen. We are Christians. Christ must be our teacher. You know his baptism.

Let your feet be washed by him. Do not ponder, do not think about it, but rather follow what I teach you. As truly as the first came about, just as certainly will the second also come. I have nothing further to say."

L...h returned again to his village and made efforts to unveil the puzzling aspect of his task. For a long time he sought in vain, and even when he thought he had found something, his reason bristled against it. "In the brain", he said; "sits the mind and I am directed to my feet. I cannot grasp it and hence I am losing hope of arriving at the goal. And yet! Was not the first teaching just as incomprehensible and nonetheless it proved its worth. The second must likewise be confirmed if I do not stand in the way obstructing myself. The plant grows from below upwards, everything which strives for security fixes itself to the ground. Steadfastness is for us only in solid materials, and what is more solid than the earth which moves irrevocably in its own circle and gives every growing creature the standpoint for its growth? The human stands on his feet, on these he supports himself; if the supports are not suited for anything, then he is lost. I must gain it and should dare everything."

L...h as Student

For six months he had to struggle, in the seventh he came to Herdtmann and said, "My feet are clean."

The latter undertook a few tests of him in order to convince himself whether all was true. He found it confirmed and gave L...h the promise to provide him soon with a new task.

Several days passed before he got involved in a conversation with L...h. He seemed even to be evading a discussion over these topics. But L...h urged him not to put his impatience to the test any longer and to take the veil from his eyes.

Herdtmann: "What should I do?"

L...h: "Give me certainty."

Herdtmann: "Have you not guessed at it yet?"

L...h: "It still lies distant from me."

Herdtmann: "Then it will be difficult to get you there so quickly."

L...h: "I will not shy from the effort. I am also not afraid of any trouble. Even bodily pains cannot scare me off. Hence I expect that you will comply with my wish."

Herdtmann: "It is done. Only with pure hands can you approach the holy one. Are your hands pure?"

L...h: "I have not done anyone violence and not damaged anyone's property. Does it need any other purity?"

Herdtmann: "You have found the end point of your life; now seek also the other parts.

The hands must come alive; when they have, then come again."

Herdtmann left. L...h gazed after him in astonishment. "He offers me one key after another; I see far before me a new world, and cannot yet enter."

He went back patiently to his village and thought to himself, "What has succeeded for me twice will also not fail the third time. Indeed the journey goes slow, but by and by I am seeing that it leads to the goal."

After three months he came this time already to his friend and addressed him in the following way, "I cannot yet indeed lay hands like our paragon on the sick and say, 'be well!', but they are coming alive." Herdtmann tested the truth of this statement and gave him on the next day the following information.

"From the day of the washing of feet to the death on the cross, everything is written only for us. If we believe in a child-like way, exercise blindly, then we too will rise again. Everything which the great master encountered in those three days is a model for us. We must feel the blows to the back and experience the torture, must bear the burden of the cross and, in order to give the new human space, spread weariness through all our limbs. Though reason may bristle against it, the senses rebel, even our entire nature become incensed, we must not waver, must endure steadfastly in order to transform the crown of pain into a crown of life. Someone who does not make many words, but puts those few words in actions everywhere, and thereby raises his entire nature to the ability of thinking, they walk the path to victory and will be glorified on the cross of life.

I have said much, less would perhaps have been better, but I am relying on you. If you persist, then I have done well. But if you do not achieve it and stop half way, then I must condemn myself that I did not proceed with care. With heavy heart I part from you this time, for many struggles await you. But, it has happened! You are thrown out into the floods; now it will be shown whether you can swim like a man or be subjected to the storms."

Herdtmann offered him his hand, kissed his cheek with a sort of melancholy and raised his eyes full of fervour to the heavens as if he were pleading for protection from above for his friend. L...h was involuntarily seized; a mood came over him like he had never had in his life before. Finally he said in great enthusiasm, "I want to reach the goal, even if it were yet so arduous to attain. The old had vanished, the new we must become. You are moved, seem to be afraid for me, but I am not hesitating. Your interest gives me strength, it encourages me for all the struggles; and even if they are yet so violent, I will think: a friend lives who worries about me, who rejoices in my happiness and shares my suffering. Rely on me! I will not deceive your trust, as truly as the feeling of love which you show me in this moment fills me with great joy and strength."

Now they parted, as inwardly stirred as you can ever be in a lifetime.

L...h arrived again in his village and thought about everything his friend has said. It stood mysteriously before his soul, but he could not doubt anymore with so many tests. "Practice makes the master", he said to himself; "what has proven itself so often, what the first, the wisest men found to be true, will also be confirmed in me. Good! Through uninterrupted, increased practice I want to seek to penetrate through the darkness."

Thus it happened too. Fifteen months he had to struggle in order to fulfill everything. Finally he obtained light, he could by and by part the darkness which his entire being was caught up in, and bring it into order. The time, although in constant struggle with himself and with all the elements of nature and of life, passed quickly for him and with the first day of the sixteenth month he greeted his friend as if he had only parted from him the day before.

Herdtmann looked at him intently and with pleasure. "Welcome!", he cried; "I see in your face that you remained true to me. Well done! From now on every wall between us falls. You are not a student anymore, you are my friend who can hold sway over me. Indeed not all the storms are over yet, but, after you attained victory, they are merely exercises for the experienced fighter. Stay now for some time with me and begrudge me the refreshment of being permitted to express myself in the nearness of a friend and to discuss with him the most sublime subjects of our existence."

From now on they lived as brothers. Every word which they spoke, even if it seemed to refer to everyday things, had for them a higher significance; for they had flown up above the everyday life and everything was to them teaching and outflow of the spirit, that eternal power which works and rules eternally in the human as in the universe.

A month had flown by in this way when Herdtmann made the suggestion of visiting their friend. L...h was content to and after a small breakfast they started on their way. When Wandorf saw them, he called out joyfully, "Welcome to these heights! The human belongs in the heights who has a triumph to celebrate. I see here approaches a victor, and hence I call out once more, welcome here to God's free temple!!"

Herdtmann offered him his hand in delight and said, "It is ours!"

Professor: "That I thought straightaway, that he would not stand still anymore once he had found the trail."

Herdtmann: "He attained it, and on this hill he shall be raised and learn to vanquish death."

They spoke still more in this sense; L...h, as deeply as he has already penetrated, could though not yet interpret all their words, and was full of expectation for the enlightenment which would be provided to him here.

After they had been together for about quarter of an hour, Herdtmann said, "Here, distant from the world, where no breath of everyday life touches the air, to which the sound of the coveting masses does not penetrate, listen here to the last doctrine.

You have received the baptism, have purified yourself from your forehead to the soles of your feet, you have penetrated into your inner-being and have recognised how arduous the journey to the cross is. So listen now!

The spirit goes in and out in the body of the human. Consolidation of it is our goal. Anyone who promotes its entry does good, but someone who learns to detain it in themselves had done something better. The nail marks of the crucified are new entrances which make contact with the innermost being of the human and form the spirit's rays into a life sun in whose light we can see and grasp everything. Open these marks and will be astonished at the love of the eternal creator."

L...h listened and, in that he had thought about what he had heard, the new entrances had already opened.

"We are formed for the cross", Herdtmann continued. "The head of the plant is in the earth, the animal's head hangs horizontally, the human has straightened up and reaches with his roots into the realm of spirits. The cross, however, fixes everything which it takes into itself. Unveil this, then the inscription which stands above the head will become clear to you. The cross in all its positions and forms is your banner. It protects and teaches you wherever you wander, because it draws the power of the spirit to itself and makes it your own.

One more thing. The number of apostles is twelve, the number of wise men or evangelists is four, but three is the eternal number. Now you know everything, if you are diligent; without exercise the best doctrine is useless."

They remained the entire day on the hill. The Professor sought to feed them as best as he could. Herdtmann's heart gushed with joy, he recited poems full of sublime content and sang songs which he elicited in enthused hours from the spirit.

Thus the hours passed. As they took their leave of the Professor, Herdtmann said, "The present day is one of those which God gives in order to show us how welcome to him joy is. It was a high feast day which should remain in our memories for evermore. Wherever we will wander on the earth, this small, but divine planet, we will think of this day and embrace each other and stay united. May in the future even lands separate us, in this place, on this hill our innermost thoughts should meet and reinforce the bond of love which embraces us now."

"Amen!", said the Professor and shook the hands of L...h and Herdtmann. Herdtmann seized them both and said, "We are united and one, and want to remain so for time and eternity!"

They parted. Night had already fallen when Herdtmann and L...h arrived home. They enjoyed a small supper and then took themselves to bed full of the emotions of the present day.

L...h remained for eight days with Herdtmann. On the ninth day he said, "It is time that I went to work, for much is assigned to me and I suspect much is still to be attained."

For five years he lingered in his village in incessant activity. A few times he visited his friends for one or at most two days. Finally he felt, even if not perfect, somewhat matured and consulted with his friends over his future way of life.

The Professor said, "Move into seclusion, there you are safe from all temptation." But Herdtmann responded, "You should not place your light under a bushel˟. We both have distanced ourselves from humanity because we are weak; L...h, however, must make the attempt in the world and see how a Christian looks amongst the wolves. The path is difficult, but he has developed a power which guarantees him safety. The world will perhaps learn from him that it is still possible to obtain the better thing, and if he only succeeds with two, then he has cancelled any debt and obtained the certainty of his reward."

They could not oppose these words in any way and L...h decided to take up residence in the great trading city of H...g.

I will pass over the events and discussions of the final days which he spent with Herdtmann and follow him to his new place of residence, where he found how difficult it is to remain true to yourself in the whirl of the world, in this great realm of blindness.

***

˟ [Tr.: cf. Matthew 5:14–15, Mark 4:21–25, and Luke 8:16–18.]

L...h in H...g

After L...h had parted from his friends, he visited his home town in order to make the necessary arrangements for his future upkeep. It was soon dealt with and now he made his way to the place of his future residence.

He put up in a guesthouse and sought idly some quarters, far from noise, but pleasantly situated. Since he was unconcerned regarding the price, he soon found what he wished for and furnished it, indeed simply, though tastefully.

He made arrangements that he received from the landlord food and housekeeping, and apart from the time of meals and the cleaning of the room saw nobody at his place.

Straightaway in the first period his way of life stood out. A man in the prime of life, of handsome, imposing figure, rich as it seemed, but who lived entirely for himself, did not visit any society or places of pleasure, all that gave cause for various conjectures over the purpose of his residence. But since in an entire year no change in his behaviour was noted, and he was seen daily to go out once and return home again soon after, they became accustomed to him and nobody said a word anymore about his seclusion.

He continued his activity with great zeal, as his profession of business, and finally achieved such clarity that he saw into the near and far, indeed into the future. The rooms of his inner life had been as it were unlocked for him so that he could transport himself at any minute into the spiritual state without changing his external posture even in the slightest.

Thus equipped, the spirit finally drove him to have an influence in public life and soon showed him a reason to.

***

L...h as Helper

One day, when he had just sat down to lunch, he stared at the wall opposite, stood up quickly, took money with him, hurried down the stairs, and asked his landlords the way to Löwen Street. They described the way to him, he recalled already having been there, went and took quick steps to a house whose number he had looked at previously. Three flights up he heard a din; he hurried up and found there a family in tears, who were about to have their possessions seized and taken away.

"What is happening here?", he asked the people. A rough voice, it was the voice of the bailiff, answered, "The riff-raff cannot pay, hence their junk is being taken."

L...h: "Who much do they owe?"

Bailiff: "Fifty talers."

L...h: "Here it is."

Bailiff: "Plus twelve groschen wages for my people."

L...h also gave this.

Bailiff: "And also two talers fine for the unruliness of not having paid straightaway at the first demand."

L...h pondered for a few moments, then paid likewise and said, "Bring the property back to its place." The bailiff replied, "Our matter is to take away, but not to put back." L...h ordered, "In with everything which you dragged out, or, by heavens, you shall get it!"

As if struck by lightning they lent a hand and in a few minutes everything stood again in it previous place. "Now away!", L...h said. They went off grumpily. He called the bailiff back and asked him, "Are you a Christian?"

Bailiff: "Yes."

L...h: "What is the first duty of the Christian?"

Bailiff: "To pray diligently and go to church every Sunday and feast day."

L...h: "The first duty of the Christian is to exercise compassion for friend and foe."

Bailiff: "As much as the office allows."

L...h: "You are prosperous?"

Bailiff: "Heaven has blessed me."

L...h: "Who receives the two talers fine?"

Bailiff: "The authorities."

L...h: "Is that certain?"

The bailiff became upset, but answered, after he had collected himself, with harsh voice, "I do not have to give anyone an accounting but the authorities."

L...h: "Good, then accompany me to the mayor."

Bailiff: "Why?"

L...h: "In order to see to whom the two talers belong."

Bailiff: "Go wherever you like, I am going my own way."

L...h took his hat to leave; the bailiff did not seem to trust him and said something more supple, "The mayor is at the town hall now and cannot give you a hearing."

"The will be seen," L...h replied and made anew as if to go. The bailiff held him back again and said, "You will cause yourself and me embarrassment."

L...h: "That does not concern me. I just want to show the high magistrate what people he puts his trust in."

Bailiff: "What, sir?!"

L...h: "You are heaping deceit on top of hard-heartedness; for the two talers are for your pocket."

Bailiff: "You dare to say such insults to a man in public service?!"

L...h: "In short, you will hand over the two talers to this family, or go with me to the mayor."

Bailiff: "Well now, if it must be, then I can be generous too. To please you; but on my honour! Anyone else would not have been permitted to make such a demand on me."

He placed the two talers on the table and said, as he was about to leave, "God be with you! Another time sort your business better, for I am not in such a good mood every day."

L...h: "Do not sin anymore!"

Bailiff: "I will take care."

L...h: "The first injustice which you further commit will also be your last."

Bailiff: "What shall be shall be. Once more, God be with you!"

The family who were supposed to have lost everything had been standing up to now in a corner of the room and did not know how it had happened. Now they approached L...h and thanked him with tears. The woman said, "You are an angel whom God sent to assist us in our undeserved misfortune."

L...h asked them to pull themselves together and to tell him in what manner they had fallen into this embarrassment.

The man said, "With poor people one misfortune immediately draws another after it. We are parents of five children. Gustav our eldest son is abroad; reckless comrades led him astray and brought him to the point where he saw no way out anymore than to be recruited into the marines. He soon saw the consequences of his blindness and wrote a heart-rending letter in which he asked us to forgive him and buy him out. What do you not do for the love of your children? We pulled together our last cash and sent it away to free him. This unforeseen expense, although it hurt us, would still not have pulled us under, but the house at which I was working as a cutler went bankrupt and did not set right my work accounts for the last half year. After that I became ill and could not look around for other work for two months. Thus it came that we were not in a position to pay the rental for our apartment. The landlord, an unfriendly man, did not want to have patience any longer and called the bailiff to assist."

L...h looked at all of them in a row, gave them eight more talers and said, "Not I, but a higher power whose instrument I am has helped you. Never forget that and it will grow blessings for you from this hour, but if you dispense with your thanks, then the misfortune will come and no helper will appear for you."

He departed, went home and admired the guidance of God which is so close to the human, but is comprehended by the fewest.

***

L...h by the Sickbed

He lived for half a year undisturbed. The cutler's family had indeed told their neighbours much about him, but they did not know his name, and hence even the curious could not find and worry him.

Seven months after these events L...h saw for two evenings in a row a face which he did not know how to interpret. A contorted face was pleading him for help, but fled timidly when he wanted to approach. "What is that?", he thought. Now he went deeper inside himself, and sort to investigate the place and circumstances. Then he recognised the house and street in which the face was to be found.

The following morning he went out in good time to obtain certainty over the spirit he had seen. For a long time he wandered fruitlessly from street to street, finally it drew him sideways and the indicated house lay before him.

He pondered for a while and thought about what was to be done here. Then he stepped into the house and asked whether an unfortunate one resided here? — "An unfortunate one? No!", was the answer; "A sinner lies on their death bed and cannot die. If you perhaps mean them, then climb up just two flights and you will see for yourself."

"What is it?", he asked himself. "Am I then blind that I cannot interpret here? But the spirit did not show me the image in vain, I must see what it is."

He climbed the stairs, but found nobody on the landing. He saw the entrances to several rooms and knocked on the one in which he believed he would find information. A quiet "Come in!" was called out. He opened the door and look! From a bed a man stared at him who at his site let out a scream of horror. He approached him; the man became more and more fearful and turned his face whimpering to the wall.

"Who are you?", L...h asked. "Do you know me, that you are frightened of me?"

The ill man: "You are my evil spirit who brought me into this miserable state."

L...h: "You are wrong, I have never seen you before."

The ill man: "You, who see everything, should not have seen me, do not know me anymore?"

L...h went inside himself and at once it became clear to him. "You are the bailiff," he said; "to whom I announced that his first deceit would also be the last. I regret that you did not listen to my warning; now the punishment has reached you."

Bailiff: "It has happened, I cannot change it anymore. Or are you perhaps in the position to help me like that cutler whom you tore from my claws? No, for me there is no helping anymore, even death does not want me for its prey!"

L...h: "Calm down and tell me how you came into this state."

Bailiff: "For five months your warning scared me and I kept myself pure of any deceit. One morning I was called, temptation arrived and indeed so enticing that I could not withstand it and a poor widow's money flowed into my pockets. But hardly had the deed been committed than the punishment followed. I hurried down the stairs in order to call my people, when I fell and broke two ribs. Like lightning it went through my brain: God has judged you! I was brought home and took a course of treatment. The visible damage seemed to heal, only in my soul a poison of hell was raging. God has judged you! This thought penetrated my entire being and brought about a fever in which I spoke constant nonsense. The fever has also vanished, but the poison remains in me and burrows into my innards. The doctors have given up on me because they cannot fathom my illness; people flee from me because I have constantly persecuted and deceived them. Now I am abandoned and have no prospects other than ending shamefully and looking to eternity without hope."

L...h took his hand as if he wanted to feel the pulse, and said, "You are truly unfortunate, for your suffering touches the innermost strings of life. Have you no family?"

Bailiff: "Yes."

L...h: "And yet you are alone?"

Bailiff: "I was too grumpy; nobody could get along with me."

L...h: "You have then children?"

Bailiff: "Yes."

L...h: "Where are they?"

Bailiff: "With their mother?"

L...h: "Do they live in this town?"

Bailiff: "Yes."

L...h: "Have they never inquired after you or visited you in your illness?"

Bailiff: "They had a mind to; I refused them."

L...h: "I want to fetch them."

Bailiff: "No."

L...h: "Why not?"

Bailiff: "Should I yet here their reproaches over my usury on my deathbed?"

L...h: "I will fetch them and foresee that it is the only means against your illness, the only way out for rescuing you from complete downfall."

L...h had himself directed to their residence and found mother and children together. He had little effort in convincing them to follow him and before an hour had passed they were by the sickbed of the husband and father.

The ill man sobbed loudly when he saw them, and for a long time he could not pull himself together; finally he reached his hand out to his wife and stammered, "I am not worthy of being in your vicinity."

L...h now made arrangements so that the ill man was not left alone anymore. He handed over the household to the wife and ordered the children to treat their father with love. But to him, the ill man, he said, "I have revealed your future to you once, now I want to say again what will happen. If you are patient, if you learn to endure, if you make yourself capable of rewarding love with love, and decide as much as possible to make good what you have perpetrated, then I lay my hand on you and pronounce that you will be healthy when the fifth day has passed."

He left and praised the miracles of the almighty who performed them through his creations.

The ill man was deeply shaken and vowed to fulfill everything. After an hour he fell into a deep sleep. On awakening he looked around himself, fortified, and said, "The poison is gone from my innards." He did indeed have a few violent attacks which were more painful than dangerous. His family attended to him warmly and competed in caring for him. On the sixth day he felt so well that he could spend five hours out of bed, the next day went still better and soon he saw himself completely recovered.

He gave up his office and sought to earn a living in a quiet business which he used for the well-being and the education of his children.

All his acquaintances were struck by the quick recovery and the complete change in his behaviour, and they asked why and from what. But as much as the family concerned told of these wondrous events, L...h though remained unknown, and you found yourself tempted to repeat the saying, "The light shines in the darkness."

***

The Interrupted Suicide

L...h had found a path for his walks which was extremely rarely visited. One day he saw a well-dressed man walking in front of him who was making strange gestures and often speaking loudly to himself. L...h doubled his attention and thought, 'What will come of this?' He kept back so as not to be noticed by the stranger. The latter became more and more vehement, his words sounded like reproaches, finally he stood still, drew a pistol from his pocket, and said, "See, thus I take revenge on you, you unthankful human race." In the moment that he began to turn the weapon towards himself, L...h called out with a strong voice, "Stop! Just a word before you shoot."

The man looked around in shock and seemed uncertain whether he should direct the pistol at himself or at L...h. The latter called out once more, "Stop!", and the other man stuck his pistol in his pocket.

Meanwhile they had come quite close to each other and the stranger asked, "What do you desire from me?"

L...h: "Information over a single question."

Stranger: "Well?"

L...h: "Are you inclined to answer?"

Stranger: "If the question is one I like."

L...h: "That is not enough; I am desiring an unconditional promise."

Stranger: "Then ask."

L...h: "What concern is the world to you?"

Stranger: "None."

L...h: "You have answered with a lie; this does not count."

Stranger: "Why not?"

L...h: "Because it runs contrary to your promise."

Stranger: "I did not lie; the world is no concern of mine."

L...h: "And yet you have the intention of leaving it?"

Stranger: "Because it is repugnant to me, because I hate it, despise it."

L...h: "As I said, you answered with a lie; for what we hate and despise is very much still of concern to us."

Stranger: "What is supposed to be the purpose of these words?"

L...h: "They instruct."

Stranger: "I do not need any instruction anymore, for my account is closed."

L...h: "With whom have you closed your account?"

Stranger: "With the world."

L...h: "Also with yourself?"

Stranger: "If I am at an end with the world, I must also be at an end with myself."

L...h: "That is not yet decided. What does the human owe to himself?"

Stranger: "That he lives as long as he wants, and then closes the account when he no longer gets pleasure from living."

L...h: "By what does the human recognise the displeasure in his life?"

Stranger: "When it gives him nothing but a bad mood."

L...h: "Life cannot give any bad mood, because it suffices of itself; only the surroundings of it touch us often strangely, and because these do not always direct us to ourselves, the bad mood comes."

Stranger: "Where is this supposed to lead?"

L...h: "To show you that our annoyance does not come from within, but rather from without. Certainly it nestles often in our heart and makes us anxious, shy, and sullen; only life itself still has no direct part in that. Tell me, gold mixed with a small amount of other metals, has it just the same value as when it is pure?"

Stranger: "No."

L...h: "But if you separate them from it?"

Stranger: "Then it has its true value again."

L...h: "Do you believe that it is different with life?"

Stranger: "Can you remove the rubbish from it when it daily mixes with other rubbish again?"

The Interrupted Suicide

L...h: "Just as little as you could purify gold if you constantly gave a new mixture again."

Stranger: "Your metaphor is thus useless!"

L...h: "I don't believe so. It'd have to be a bad laboratory technician who, when he was purifying gold, at the same moment let it be contaminated again."

Stranger: "The effort to purify gold rewards itself; with life that is not the case."

L...h: "You are deceiving yourself because you have lost the courage for purification. Make an attempt for once and you will find how precisely the metaphor fits."

Stranger: "I do not dispute your claim, but rather the value of it."

L...h: "Life is the highest thing in nature! Anyone who purifies it has done the highest thing which the human is in a position to perform."

Stranger: "Anyone who has the courage to lose the highest is elevated above fear and doubt and has thereby obtained the first prize."

L...h: "You are looking at the matter from the wrong side. That is just as much as if someone said that in order to have something, you must have nothing. You see on what wrong pillars your principles stand."

Stranger: "That is for the human the highest thing which he recognises for it."

L...h: "When it is examined, admittedly; but who gives the greatest value to an uncertain state which shows that he is blind and entertains chance?"

Stranger: "From chance comes everything we possess."

L...h: "The sun has its ordered course, the host of stars moves to a wonderful eternal rule. To raw material a law is given, and life should be without plan?"

Stranger: "My answer is final and my rule is: everybody do as they like."

L...h: "That is the most complete law of human nature that everybody decides as they like and chooses what is best for them. Anyone who chooses well is chosen; one who chooses foolishly must atone themselves for their foolishness."

Stranger: "What is the point of this idle talk?"

L...h: "To teach you that it is wrong when we decide blindly and step just as blindly towards the execution. Allow me one more question: what would you say of a man who, because someone mixed his gold with other metals, now threw it in the sea?"

Stranger: "I would call him a fool."

L...h: "What would you call someone who did that only to annoy an enemy?"

Stranger: "He would be in my eyes a fool twice over. Firstly because he threw away his possessions, and secondly because he thereby only fulfilled the intention of his enemy."

L...h: "Well said. Do you not feel that in your answer lies your own judgement?"

Stranger: "It has some similarity with my position. But if the wealth is a burden, can he do something better than throw it away?"

L...h: "Yes. He can become rational and think that he who has something is to be appraised as more fortunate than he who possesses nothing. But enough over this point. Whoever wants to be a fool is one; I seek to preserve what is accorded to me, and in the end it will be shown whether I have not done well."

Stranger: "Who will call you to account over it?"

L...h: "Nature, our mother; God, our judge."

Stranger: "There is no God."

L...h: "There is a God, as true as you will kick a stone in five days at the big market square and injure your foot."

Stranger: "Who? Me? I take the bet. If it happens, then I must believe that you have me in bond and can lead me like a child is led."

L...h: "I lead no one; providence does it, and good for those who feel its hand and like to follow its guidance."

L...h left. The stranger stood in doubt as to whether he had held this conversation while awake or dreaming. "In five days I will injure my foot?", he said. "A bad prophecy! If I fire the pistol at my brain then he has spoken into the wind! — But, my mood is different than an hour ago! In five days I will give the matter some thought anew."

Slowly he returned to the town. He could barely await the time and had already avoided the way across the market square for four days. "What I was capable of before", he thought, "will not be impossible for me tomorrow either."

On the evening of the fourth day he was in company. As he was walking home late, it occurred to him that he could shame his prophet the most securely if he left the town and spent a day in the countryside. He went to the gates to desire to be let out; there he at once became so unwell that he was forced to walk home. The shortest way led him across the big market square. "It is not yet the fifth day", he said to himself; "so straight ahead." As he made this decision, he became so ill that he had to sit down on a stone. Now it struck midnight. The fateful day had begun. He pulled himself together, his feet trembled, in his innards a violent pain was raging, he hurried mindlessly across the square and struck his foot on a stone so hard that he could not stand on his left foot anymore and was forced to lie down on the cobbles.

At this moment a strong hand seized him to hold him upright and to lead him home. "Who is it who comes to help in my need?", he asked. "The one who told you five days ago that there is a God!", answered L...h who had foreseen what would happen in this hour.

Stranger: "You spoke the truth, I feel the proof in my pain. But what led you here? How could you know that right now..."

L...h: "The power which showed me what would happen to you also unveiled to me the time. But about that another time! Here we must not linger; support yourself on me so that I can get you to your residence."

The injured man felt so weak on his feet that he had to be more carried than led. Finally they made it, without causing a stir, to his room where L...h had him lie down to unclothe him and see to the damage. He took a cloth and bound it around the injured foot and said, "In two days you will be sound and on the third I expect to see you on the pathway we know."

Thus it also happened. When the stranger saw him there again, he went up to him and said, "It is a God who rules the world and us. You have placed the seed in me, will you protect it against the storms and sunshine, and against the poisonous army of insects?"

L...h: "I will protect it if you remain steadfast and want to obtain clarity in yourself about humanity's highest good, life."

The man handed himself over to L...h's guidance. It would be long-winded to describe the entire course of education which he had to walk through, only so much must be said, that he obtained a fondness for life and learned to consider it to be the single goal of human ennoblement. L...h wrote to Herdtmann amongst other things the following about him: "He stood in the darkest nigh, on the edge of the eternal death; now he sees the new heavens and rejoices at the sight of its stars."

***

Public Works

L...h's effectiveness, as much as it also seemed hidden, became know by and by, and gave cause for new suspicions. His name, to which you paid no heed previously, seemed now to be at once well-known because his father stood in business connections with the most significant local houses and he himself had acquired some reputation as a scholar. The business people and scholars now wanted to obtain precise information about his person and his family in order to then get to know him better and become clear about the wondrous stories which were in circulation about him.

The reports that arrived gave unanimous testimony that he was the one whom they suspected and everybody now endeavoured to do pay him their respects and do him favours.

L...h had already long since foreseen a change in his way of life, regardless of which he was surprised by the crowd of visitors and their showing of courtesies.

"The spirit wants me to go out into the world," he said to himself, "well, it shall guide and protect me."

There existed in H...g an association of scholars which in three days was celebrating its founding, and inviting guests from all the educated classes from near and far. L...h was also suggested and a delegation of three members undertook to expressly deliver the invitation to him.

The delegation, consisting of the general practitioner Doctor Wilding, the legal scholar Kirkner, and the writer Ruhland, came to his apartment and asked in the name of the association for the honour of his taking part in the celebration of their founding.

L...h replied to this courtesy with appropriate thanks, sought to decline the invitation, however, because he could not count himself amongst the class of scholars of Germany.

They responded to him that too much modesty was not a good thing; also they did not consider it right from his side that he had remained hidden for so long and was burying his talents as it were. That had to change now, the writer suggested, and Kirkner, the legal scholar, who imagined himself to be a great dialectician, made the remark that it was his and every scholar's duty to draw forth the talent and to give it the opportunity to let its light shine.

L...h made no further objections and accepted the invitation. Kirkner requested the honour of being permitted to fetch him and introduce him to the gathering.

On the specified day the legal scholar came and brought L...h to the gathering, which was extremely numerous and brilliant. At the unaccustomed sight of so many people a spontaneous anxiety crept up on L...h, but it soon passed. He quickly composed himself, surveyed the crowd with calm eyes and let himself be introduced by his companion to the chair of the festivities, the mayor Schöppmann. The latter received him with decorum, regretted that one had not gotten to know him previously and could only now give him evidence of the hospitality which was a characteristic of the local residents. "But what we have neglected", he continued; "will yet be made up for. Doctor Kirkner, I ask that you take care that our guest leaves with the honour he deserves."

As soon as the table was arranged, they sat down. L...h was granted the distinction of taking his place in the vicinity of the committee. He was in a strange mood. The din, the many words which swirled about his ears, awoke in him the fear that his inner-being could be drowned out by it. He therefore made a few attempts with himself and found that the spirit was not bound to any place, nor to any circumstances. Now he was confident and abandoned himself entirely to his happy mood. After the meal toasts were drunk. Doctor Kirkner also gave one to L...h's health and praised with a great torrent of words their luck in having amongst themselves the greatest dialectician of the age. He summoned the gathering to attend to his joy in order to enable such a guest to show his talents publicly and to found a private school in their town. Everybody agreed, even the mayor in the end took up the discussion and said, "There is indeed no university here, only we honour the sciences and encourage those who seek to spread them amongst us. In the name of the city council and the entire town I give you herewith not only the permission to erect a school, but ask you to do so, with the assurance that we will be thankful for it in word and deed."

L...h felt strangely seized when he heard this request; the words of Herdtmann occurred to him: when you enrich your matter with eternal laws, you build altars for humanity. — "Here would be the opportunity", he thought; "to make an attempt, but I must be cautious." He also asked now for permission to speak. His soul swelled up when he stood up to speak. "Formerly", he said to himself; "I was speaking learned phrases, now my inner-being shall speak from me."

To set down his entire talk would not be allowed by the space of these pages; but a few principle features must not remain untouched. After he gushed in thanks and held forth appropriately on the essence of the usual dialectics, he continued, "Philosophy, what is it? I have practised it according to the given propositions and when the given was at an end, I found myself in the lurch. I looked around in history in order to seek philosophers who were on the trail of the essence and penetrated arduously into the innermost core; and there I discovered that our current philosophical systems are only the frameworks of those sublime models, and I did not rest until I too had penetrated the inner-being of my science. The spirit of philosophy stems from eternity! Time gave the framework. — Out of the eternal sea of thoughts it must flow if it should possess independence. Hence forgive me that I cannot decide so easily to erect a public school when I do not know whether you desire the thing or just the adornment. I will remain amongst you; if someone who possesses the courage finds themselves gazing into eternity, they will be my student. For the outward appearance, for the surroundings of philosophy, I cannot be a teacher anymore now that I have recognised its depths."

In this way he dissected his views and concluded his talk amidst the loudest calls of jubilation from the assembled audience.

The company parted. Doctor Kirkner accompanied him home. He gave him the assurance that everybody had been delighted over his behaviour and each would endeavour to sign up first if he was of a will to undertake something. "Your fortune is made," he said; "if you make use of this mood; for our town is rich and likes to give when you bring it a few sacrifices." L...h replied that he would consider it and share his thoughts about it with him in due course.

Kirkner left. L...h was happy to be alone. His external senses, not accustomed to such large gatherings anymore, were exhausted and he needed a good while until he had collected himself again.

It was not so calm in the town; everybody had to talk about the stranger, about his behaviour, about his figure, about the sound of his voice, but mainly about the content of his talk which, although understood by few, left behind though a forceful impression. In a few of the listeners the wish had already arisen to come into closer contact with him in order to receive from him instruction over his views face to face or at least in a smaller circle.

Already the next morning L...h received a visit from a general practitioner by the name of Lutweg, who according to the custom of the time connected theosophy with medicine. After the usual greetings he came out straightaway with it and said, "Good sir, you developed in your talk yesterday views which I have suspected for a long time, but could not get clear in my mind. Your depictions of a higher nature and of a purer philosophy were so succinct that I consider myself convinced they were not mere phrases, but rather produced from inner conviction, and if that is so, then I ask you to consider me worthy of being given proper enlightenment over those subjects!"

L...h: "You have thought things over quickly."
Doctor: "Time passes quick."
L...h: "We must hold on to it."
Doctor: "How is that possible?"
L...h: "Name our every moment."
Doctor: "In my professional business that does not work."
L...h: "Everywhere."
Doctor: "I cannot believe it."

L...h: "The essence of God is everywhere; no place, no time, no business can separate us from it. In it is everything which we are and do."

Doctor: "Quite right. If we know and feel it, then it is true; but when we are often not in command of our thoughts, what then?"

L...h: "The thought must be in command. It is presumptive to want to dominate it. Presumption is sin. When we are afraid of sin, then we are always in the being of God."

Doctor: "I cannot grasp that; but I believe it. Do not abandon me, and allow me to come again."

L...h: "Very good."

The doctor took his leave and went to his patients. But L...h thought, "If the man had time for living, then he could learn to live, but there is no hope of that."

In the afternoon the high school teacher Bielhorst came to visit and wanted, like the previous man, to be led into the realm of that eternal philosophy where it shone as bright light of wisdom.

"Have you courage?", said L...h.

Teacher: "If it is needed."

L...h: "Give me proof of it."

Teacher: "How can I do that?"

L...h: "If you show me that you keep your composure in the moment when it is about life and death."

Teacher: "I do not understand you."

L...h: "You must know that I am a soldier for truth and do not let myself be easily deceived. You want to shake from a different tree because you yourself are only a little branch which bears no fruit. Let this little branch grow until it can stand without support, then come again to me."

Bielhorst looked at him in consternation. "What language are you speaking? You are accusing me of deceit in that I ask for instruction. Is that right?"

L...h: "I know you. You will end up where you belong. Only one thing can save you: repent!"

Teacher: "What should I repent for?"

L...h: "For your perverse teachings. For your intention of giving pretence instead of truth and of shining in order to increase your income. You want to borrow a shimmer from me in order to raise yourself yet more and to press your sceptre even harder on your subordinates."

Teacher: "Those are injuries which I will not let drop."

L...h: "Act as you like. I will say only one thing to you: if you want to sue me, then do it soon, for before you suspect it, your hour has come."

Bielhorst went away furious. He did not indeed have the courage to make a formal complaint, but found creatures who connected with him to arouse suspicion of L...h where they could.

L...h noticed the game which was being played out in the darkness, but he could not and was not permitted to hinder it. "I have shown myself publicly and must expect whatever will come upon me."

In the following days he received still more visits, almost each one of a different type. One wanted to make himself important with him, another sought to question him, a third had been serious to learn something from him if it could have occurred with little effort; but most wanted only to be know for also having spoken to him face to face.

Made attentive by the stories which were spreading in the town about L...h's characteristics and wondrous gifts, all the unfortunates and ill obtained an unbounded trust in him. Where help was needed, he was sought, when the doctors no longer knew how to save a patient, refuge was taken in him. A poor sufferer from gout, because he wanted only to be handed over to his treatment, was brought to him. He looked at him for a few moments and asked, "What do you want here?"

Patient: "To become well."

L...h: "In what way?"

Patient: "However the master decides."

L...h: "You are speaking of the master in heaven?"

Patient: "He can also help. This time I was speaking of one by the name of L...h."

L...h: "Do you know him?"

Patient: "No."

L...h: "I am him."

Patient: "Good! Then I will soon be helped."

L...h: "If it happens, who will have done it?"

Patient: "God."

L...h: "Not I?"
Patient: "No. God through you."
L...h: "Why do you not go to others?"
Patient: "They do not know God, cannot ask him, cannot speak to him."
L...h: "Why do you not speak to him?"
Patient: "Oh lord, if I could, then I would never be ill for evermore."
L...h: "Good! Then listen, in two days you will be well. But now go where you can rest."

The patient was led home and in two days was well.

L...h possessed the gift of unveiling the hidden and bringing to light crimes to a high degree.

He uncovered one thief in the following way. A young man, who was accused of theft and already considered guilty of it, although he had not yet confessed anything himself, shall have been placed in the pillory as a deterring example for his deed and his stubborn denial. The condemned seemed quite composed and said, when he had climbed up, "It will yet become known; now I must give way to force, but God will take up my matter."

"He has taken it up!", L...h called out loudly. "There is the thief!" — he pointed to the place where the spirit guided him to. "Up, grab him, before he escapes!"

Everybody was astounded and looked at the place where the thief was supposed to be found.

He called once more, "Up, after me! Otherwise he will escape and the innocent will accuse you of dilly dallying." He went with a few policemen to the place. Now he stopped and said to the people, "Nobody stir from this place, so that I can grab the thief undisturbed and deliver him into the hands of justice." He neared the crowd alone and look, a man who was standing in the first row and to whom he went directly, forced himself back bit by bit in order to lose himself amongst the others and escape. "Seize him who left his place", L...h said; "he is the thief." The police grabbed him and he confessed his guilt immediately. The other man was taken down from the pillory and taken home in jubilation.

Another time a stranger came to L...h and recited the following history.

"In my hometown thirty years go there lived a clerk by the name of B...r...g who was not well-liked because it was claimed he deceived the people and even did not deal with the land's accounts in an honest way. My family possessed a precious ring which has never been sold in order to have a safe guarantee for any emergency. The rumours of B...r...g's dishonest acts became louder, indeed they even said the government was getting involved with investigating his affairs, but to set a trap for him. He got wind of these attempts, put to the side as much as he could, and one morning he had vanished. Now it also happened that right on the same night our ring also went astray without the trace of any thief being found. What then was more natural that that everyone was convinced B...r...g had craftily purloined it before he took flight.

Nothing was heard of the fugitive. All efforts were indeed made to inquire as to his whereabouts, but in vain. My family, as painful as such a loss also was, had to console itself and count the ring amongst the lost goods.

Nobody thought anymore of B...r...g. Suddenly after quarter of a year a letter came from the Cape, in which a sort of sealed testament to our town council was enclosed. It was opened, and they recognised immediately B...r...g's hand and signature. It was an outline of his life in which he confessed his former deceptions and purloinings, and asked all the residents of the town for forgiveness in his final hours. We were full of expectation of learning something about our ring; but there was not a syllable of mention of it. Because we were now put in uncertainty anew, but had no trail on which to start an inquiry, I have come to you with the request to consider this matter and to give me some information about it."

L...h thought about the incident and said, "Your ring was stolen by a common crook."

Stranger: "Where is the ring to be found now though?"

L...h: "In the hands of a watch seller who intends to sell it in far-off lands."

Stranger: "And the thief?"

L...h: "Is now an old man and still fears being punished. He sold the ring for not much money only in order to get rid of it. Its current owner is also not at ease until he has disposed of it."

Stranger: "How can the rightful owners get it back?"

L...h: "You must seek out the watch seller. He is coming here in twelve days and will reside in B...n Street where you can easily discover him."

The stranger remain in H...g for twelve days. A watch seller took up quarters in the named street. In order to not cause a stir, the stranger sought to speak to him alone, and he succeeded so perfectly in his intention that he received the ring for a small outlay, and learned the name and residence of the thief. Only now did he make the matter known to the courts. The thief was arrested and yet made to pay in his old age.

L...h had many arguments with scholars, for his principles, even when they went away fully convinced by him, did not want to take root in them, and hence they made every effort to draw suspicion on his views and to bring their own into esteem.

Thus it happened that a professor from the Lyceum, by the name of Hohlwerk, who had formerly been one of his followers, but had now fallen away from him, occasionally made him explain himself and asked, "Now, my good doctor, are you still always true to your mystical doctrine?"

L...h: "Yes."

Professor: "That surprises me. Passionate enthusiasms usually soon reverse."

L...h: "So they do. What are not passionate enthusiasms accordingly advance. How far have you already advanced?"

Professor: "I have learned to see that your matter has no basis."

L...h: "To obtain this insight needs no striding forward, to the contrary, it can happen through a backward step. Listen to parable.

A man had many forests. In one forest were beech trees, in another fir trees, and in a third willow trees. Now a stranger came and desired to buy wood. 'What sort of species do you want?', the owner asked. 'Of the best', was the answer. 'Now, then I will give you beech.' The trade was concluded, the wood delivered, but in a short time the buyer came and said,

'Do you still have your bad forest? I have been instructed by someone better and learned to see that your wood is not suited for anything, it is too hard for me.'"

L...h went his way, but the Professor was too taken with his own ideas that such a gibe could hurt him. "Dreamers are the same in all times", he said to one of his friends; "you seek in vain to convince them."

A poet once said to him, "The art of poetry is of divine nature."

L...h: "Yes, when it comes from heaven."

Poet: "No, when it climbs to heaven."

L...h: "Not bad. It is a pity for you that you do not have the beginning."

Poet: "The beginning!"

L...h: "Understand me right, I mean the beginning of the thing where nothing can climb to heaven which does not come from heaven."

Poet: "I know these sayings, only they have no basis."

L...h: "Why not?"

Poet: "Because they do not make us richer, but rather turn us around in a circle where everything remains as of old."

L...h: "You would thus like to create something new?"

Poet: "Yes."

L...h: "Even in its essence?"

Poet: "of course."

L...h: "Then I must ask, how many colours are there?"

Poet: "Three primary colours; they are usually divided into seven."

L...h: "Where does the basic matter of the colours lie?"

Poet: "In nature."

L...h: "Can you increase the sorts by one, or is the quantity given?"

Poet: "That question is strange."

L...h: "No less. Listen. A rich man gathered from an entire province all the colours in stock and brought them into various rooms. But blue was his favourite colour, hence he said to his people, 'Make me more of this sort.' They answered, 'That is not possible, there is no more to be found.' But he did not relent in his desire and said, 'I am assigning you to create still more blue for me; anyone who delivers me a little shall receive a reward, but those who bring a lot, to them I will give what their heart desires.'

The people gave the matter some thought and said, 'We must fulfill our master's command. Well, we want to try to see whether blue is also contained in the other colours, and then draw out as much as is possible.' The master noticed this work and said, 'Now you have done well'; and added, 'so it is in the creation; only what comes from heaven can climb again to heaven.'"

The poet had listened attentively and said, "That is not bad, for it still leaves us freedom of action. But the matter is not to be carried out, one would otherwise have to be at the same time a theologian and an artist."

L...h: "Would that then be so wrong?"

Poet: "No, it would be good and would give art a goal which it now lacks. You have edified me, but also humbled deeply. How can poetry continue to suffice more me after this observation?"

L...h: "I do not know. But it is clear to me that not everything is gold which glitters, and when the purification follows one day, it will show who made the attempt."

They parted. The poet morosely, for he had hoped to obtain victory for his matter, and left this fight himself defeated, which he could not forget for a long time, and which drove him in the end to get to know L...h's doctrine a bit closer. How far he went with it, over that the annals are silent.

Another time someone thought he had hurt him when he criticised his doctrine. L...h said, "Your criticism does not hit me and nor my doctrine, but rather he who I explain through it." — "Who is that?", they asked. — "God!", answered L...h; "Hence in future be, even if not quiet, modest, so that the power which you do not know does not harm you."

In this way L...h carried on for two years, and the town separated into two parties, of which the one accorded him the highest admiration, while the other not only put him down, but also made every exertion to harm him and to expel him disgracefully.

The schoolmaster had already been working against him; now he made a complaint and declared him to be an enemy of religion, an atheist who bewitched his adherents with phrases and drew their hearts away from the true God.

The dean called for a report and found much in agreement with this accusation. He made the decision to take the matter to heart and to call in the accused for an examination if he continued thus.

The doctors for whom he had healed so many patients and reduced their income were easily moved to make common cause with the clergy and appear against him.

He has also a thorn in the eye of the scholars because they saw that their matter did not stand up next to him and they were overshadowed by him.

In this way by and by a party formed against him which by virtue of its members and their number was the most terrible which had ever formed against any individual. L...h saw it, but could not and was not permitted to undertaken anything against them. "What must come will come", he said to himself; "when it is time then the means will show themselves too."

Everything was ready to appear against him. It was only about submitting a formal accusation in order to bring the matter up before the court. A meeting was instituted by the accusers in order to discuss various points and to bring them into agreement.

The accusations were drafted, a masterpiece of sophistry and envy. It would be going too far to set it down here; the content was in essence the following.

The clergy declared him to be an atheist who with cleverly placed words denied religion and undermined its principles. In the eyes of the doctors he was on of those unauthorised people who crept into their subject without any knowledge, drew people to themselves through feigning miraculous powers, and spread superstition and illnesses amongst them. The scholars, that is, the professors of the Lyceum and the libellers, described his principles as inadmissible and seductive because they inflamed the imagination, poisoned the disposition, and instead of laying the foundation for a firm power of thought, filled those desiring to learn with enticing dreams and weakened their intellect.

Public Works

The mayor, who was still on L...h's side, read the accusations and was scared for him. "He is from out of town", he said to a close member of the town council; "someone who cannot abandon himself to the protection of our laws. I foresee him being lost and the least which can happen to him is banishment from our town."

The matter now went its usual prescribed course. L...h was brought in for examination and questioned in particular over every accusation. He gave short answers and insisted on defending himself before a public court according to the laws and the customs of the town. The accusers indeed did not want to allow this because he was from out of town, but the mayor decided that the honour of the town council demanded handling it publicly in such an important matter and going to work with the greatest impartiality.

The day of the hearing was set. Everybody was in tense expectation. Several suggested that putting L...h in jail until the end of the matter, but a few business people who had previously been connected with his family provided guarantees for him, and thus he looked towards the day of decision unchallenged and calm.

The hour came. The courtroom was crowded, people had even gathered in the street in order to be informed through arranged signals from the windows all the quicker of the course of the hearing and the given verdict.

The accusations were read publicly. L...h rose, and asked for permission to be allowed to defend himself; it was granted to him, after a repeated survey of the persons of the court, and he began.

"I am accused of severe crimes according to the words, but the sense of the accusations speaks more for than against me. The venerable clergy will allow that I turn to them first in my defence. They say I am an atheist and am undermining the principles of religion. I cannot talk about the entire extent of this accusation, but I must cite for my justification a few teachings which Christ himself gave and followed. He said, 'by their fruits or works you shall know them.'* Now I ask what works might he have meant here? Though not such

---
*   [Tr.: cf. Matthew 7:16.]

outward works which the sinner is capable of exercising just like the pious? Giving alms, visiting church, founding hospitals, all these the villain can do; but to live in the spirit, to act in it and to venerate God is only possible for the true Christian. They abandon themselves indeed to the words, 'Not every one that saith unto me, Lord, Lord, shall enter into the kingdom of heaven; but he that doeth the will of my Father which is in heaven.'* — Now I ask, which is the father's will? How is the human in a position to recognise it? Certainly not through our laws and forms of thought, otherwise Paul would not have agitated so much against the Greeks who in outward respects were not bad thinkers. The human must find his life in the spirit, in the rebirth he obtains the kingdom of heaven into which the sublime founder of our religion wants to lead us. Furthermore it states, 'The father wants that you pray to him in spirit and in truth.'† Only the born again is in spirit and can pray to him in it; only he who is in spirit had the prophetic power and can recognise the truth. I am in the spirit, I am thinking and acting in it, and hence I count myself amongst those who pray to the father in spirit and in truth.

One more thing. They say the time of miracles is past, with Christ the power was shut off which could lead us to the spirit which reveals itself in effectiveness. But I bring to your attention the words, 'When you follow me, you will be able to not only do this, but still greater works.'‡ — Christ is my example, I chose him to be my model and teacher, and if I perform works which are incomprehensible to other humans then those who live in the spirit and believe in Christ will find my works in accord with scripture and in complete harmony with the principles of our religion. I think enough has been said over it and hence pass on to the other accusations.

The esteemed gentlemen who through their knowledge serve the suffering part of humanity, and heal sickness with means which they owe to understanding and experience, and promote and preserve the state of help of this town, these gentlemen call me unauthorised, and say I am spreading

---

* [Tr.: Matthew 7:21.]
† [Tr.: cf. John 4:23.]
‡ [Tr.: cf. John 14:12.]

superstition and illnesses. I cannot fathom how they come to this accusation, for I have not made any healthy person ill; to the contrary, through my inner power many were pulled back from the grave when your remedies were already long since exhausted. I do not say too much when I claim that without inner knowledge the science of medicine stands on unstable ground, and the slightest deviation from the everyday must shift the doctor into uncertainty.

The reproach that I am spreading superstition I do not like to touch because it seems to me far-fetched and contains a hostility towards me which I do not deserve. I have obtained with effort what I possess, and yet I do not turn anyone away who desires something from me. I have taught and explained where it is desired, and never demanded payment and thanks for it. If I now appeared and said to the patient, 'God can help!', is that spreading superstition, or should medicine have no communion with God and stand alone without life principle, that which has its goal in the activity of life? It is enough if I deliver here the explanation that to work in God is no superstition, but to work without God is unbelief.

Over my calling to be allowed to heal illnesses there is much to be said. If the gentlemen think the doctor's diploma is the basis of the profession then I must concede to them. But if they understand a calling of a higher sort by that, where it is allowed to nobody to accept patients who has not proven themselves by trial, then I say that I believe my attempts are considered to be valid, for not one of those patients who trusted in me has died. But if this does not suffice to prove the suitability of my calling, then listen to me! Listen to me, noble gentlemen of the court! Listen to me, worthy crowd that is present! I want to prove the worth of my calling — in three days thirty patients, cured by me, shall leave the hospital and thank God for their recovery. If it does not happen, then all the complaints against me are well-founded — but if it occurs, then I have performed a work in which the Christian can recognise the Christian and the doctor the master called to it."

Deep silence reigned in the courtroom after these words. The surprise which they brought forth was so general that nobody could doubt anymore what turn the matter would take. Finally the mayor, as president of the court, rose and asked, "Does anyone have any objection to the suggested presentation of evidence by the accused?" Several individual voices wanted to be heard, but were drowned out by the noise of the crowd. The mayor continued, "Since no considerable objections have occurred, I move that the court make its way to its private room in order to put to a vote the admissibility of the suggestion." The motion was accepted and the court personnel left the room.

After half an hour they returned and read out the following speech.

"The accused doctor of philosophy, L...h from St...t by birth, thirty years old, has for two years in the present town spread his doctrine and healed the sick without having requested an authority to do so. So that this authority becomes his, he offers to heal in three days thirty patients in the local hospital. Since the high court has found this desire fair, it gives permission for it and will acquit the accused, when he has fulfilled his word, of every accusation. The college of medicine is tasked with being conducive to his attempt and to taking the necessary measures.

Given for H...g, etc."

This verdict spread like wildfire through the entire town. "It is unheard-of! Unbelievable! Thirty patients in three days!" These exclamations were heard on all the streets and in every gathering.

The doctors led L...h to the hospital, separated those who were already counted amongst the recovered from the others, and handed over to him the list of all the patients present.

As he considered the number of names, he said, "Were I perfect, like I should be, then all these could become well, but I am yet weak and capable only of having an effect on gout, limb pains, cold fever, and a few common illnesses; the greatest evils are not yet subject to me and hence I confess out loud that I am yet far from that high goal which shall one day come where the human vanquishes death."

He had himself led through all the rooms of the hospital, comforted the patients and gave them hope, and awoke such a trust amongst them that they all begged him to help them.

After he had seen all the patients, he left and went home, where he was as calm as if nothing had happened at all.

A few of his friends advised him to visit the hospital more frequently and to be alert so that no deception would take place. But he said, "Deception is impossible here; it will go as it must go and nobody can shift the course of time even by just a hair."

"But the events which happen in time", another replied; "depend upon humans." — "You are right," L...h responded; "but I am letting another keep watch for me who is not to be deceived and not to be made tired."

The third day had broken. An unusual crowd of people had assembled at the hospital. L...h appeared in the company of a few doctors. He went through the wards and called everyone to him who had become well that day. There were thirty. "Let us now go to the town hall," L...h said to them; "give testimony there for me that you were ill and since today have recovered from your maladies." They followed him and called incessant thanks and blessings to him and praised him as their saviour. The people agreed in this jubilation and his arrival at the town hall was like a triumphal procession.

The high council was assembled and confirmed its verdict. Now a new cry of joy sounded from the gathered crowd and many praised God that he also revealed himself in their days.

Those who had recovered were fed at the cost of the town, but L...h withdrew from the tumult and sat down at home at his writing desk in order to report to his friend Herdtmann over the events of these days.

He remained until his end in H...g, but withdrew more in order to not give cause for a commotion which could have become dangerous in the end.

All who knew him loved and revered him, and saw him as a phenomenon for teaching humans to again seek their better selves and thereby arrive at life.

***

Retrospective

We have started from the lowest standpoint of spiritual life, magnetism, and have considered in various gradations the powers and elaborations of the spirit.

The first sort already stands for that reason deeper because it is not free, not yet the property of the human, but rather must be brought forth by foreign influence. The freedom of the human calls for that he himself distinguishes, chooses, and decides.

The history of the journeyman joiner places us on a step where the human seeks his inner life from a certain natural urge, and finds it without outside influence but as a pure property of his ego. It is already of a higher sort because it corresponds more to the demands of human nature which under all circumstances seek to preserve its freedom and its own will.

Freedom is the purest, original property of the human. The dignity of his entire life rests in the feeling and consciousness of it. Every doctrine which seeks to take this from him finds little favour and hence orthodoxy works with so little success.

L...h lifted himself to complete freedom and hence he is for our aim an important example.

The given explanations which occur in his story indeed often seem to stand in contradiction to this freedom, only with closer inspection this freedom proves itself also in the greatest dependency.

Dependence on God is not a terrible thought for the human, to the contrary, nobody can help having this thought, and for those who devote themselves to him, he becomes a feeling of life.

Dependency and freedom seem certainly not to be united and yet they are intimately connected.

The human has the free request, God the granting. The request is unconditionally free, for the human can ask, but he can also refrain from it.

"Is the granting also free?", I hear many ask. If this is so, then the human is not anymore.

The granting is free in respect to the human, but God has forgone this freedom from the very beginning.

God has poured out his spirit into the creation for the creature. From this everybody can obtain as much as his request his capable.

Those who know to ask are certain of the granting, nothing remains shut off from them and nothing withheld, because everything is already given in advance.

We must learn to collect, to draw from that eternal sea of life which flows around us, in us, and in all the regions of creation and give to everyone as much of its inner content as they can grasp.

Salt is spread through all of nature, those who do not seek it must do without it.

Fire and light penetrate through every sphere, those who do not give it a good base and draw from firm matter have neither warmth nor light in the winter nights.

Life flows through all the regions of creation, if no procreation takes place then life cannot portray itself in its characteristics and forms.

Light of thought streams through every space and all beings, but those who do not collect it are like those who languish for thirst next on a great current.

Powers of God, of love, of wisdom, and omnipotence are everywhere; if we do not seek them they remain inactive for us and we live in want with the most previous meal of kings; we know nothing, meanwhile wisdom lives around us and in us; we sigh in weakness, meanwhile the outpoured power joins us as soon as we are in a position to win.

We must consider L...h's views in this higher sense. The inner life was for him as innate as the external gestures. With the same certainty with which he moved a hand, he walked in the spirit and set its characteristics into action, and hence his story is for our task of great worth because we see in him a development of nature which describes for us the possibility of a primal state in which the human can awaken the powers of life in clarity and freedom, and can recognise them in all respects.

The doctrines which led him to his standpoint comprise the greatest part of his story. We considered it to be expedient to enter at length it to it in order to lead the reader in a matter to a united understanding of which he usually has very erroneous ideas. We wanted to systematically show the way to a new activity which is unavoidably necessary if the human should find himself again.

The appearance of Herdtmann is thereby of significance because he had the courage to go to the root of the doctrine and to grow a strong plant only from this.

Herein lies the teaching concept: that we go to the beginning, to the cradle, where a simple stammering reveals itself, and then passes through all the stages of education to higher thought.

The first thing in life is stammering, the highest is thinking in freedom.

Free thought is the crown of life; for it recognises itself and reflects itself in itself.

But even here the human again easily comes into temptation. He would like to think and the original thought does; the human would like to have it as a tool, meanwhile he is the tool.

The thought speaks — I — the outer human has learnt it from that.

The closer the learned self comes to the inner self, the clearer our life becomes and rises to perfect clairvoyance.

This clairvoyance, this inner knowing and ruling gives back to the human his natural origin where he first obtains the true freedom.

Without this inner freedom no other is thinkable; for outside the desires and passions reign.

Without this inner freedom neither happiness nor calm can exist, because outside everything floats in worries and uncertainty.

Without it no knowledge either can illuminate us, because all outer phenomena are subject to chance which leads us constantly into new doubt and confusion.

Johann Baptist Krebs

The doctrine exists. Whoever has the desire and courage will learn from it; the timid and lazy are not worthy of any prize.

Learn to think, live, and act in yourself, then you will be safe for now and all future times.

***

A Glance into the 13th and 14th Centuries

The calm researcher uncovers traces of the spiritual life everywhere he directs his attention. No climate, no epoch comprises an exception to that eternal rule which places the human as the crown of creation and sees perfection in him. But it is no easy task to seek in all the forms in which the times and lands distinguish themselves from one another the activity of this unchangeable primal power and to reveal it historically. Only, anyone who does not shy from the effort and trusts in that inextinguishable light must in the end discover such traces on which he can walk with reasonable safety and draw truth from the darkness.

We are entering a century which appears wild and chaotic, and few threads are to be discovered which lead us out of the labyrinth if we once have dared our way into it. But as the sun also at the time warmed the lands with its light, with the same certainty we must assume that the spiritual sun spreads its influence just as effectively, and filled those who placed themselves in its light with life warmth, courage, and belief.

The thirteenth century distinguishes itself through its religious passions and sects which could not yet bring into harmony the received religion with their views and feelings, and hence incessantly endeavoured to reform for as long as until they came to some clarity.

The Inquisition formed in that time its own class, and gave history many ghastly examples of its zeal for the positive laws. The current generation damns those arrangements as the most gruesome aberrations of the human spirit, but does not consider that without that terrible institution Europe would have stood in thousands of religious forms where nobody would know anymore to whom they belonged.

We are far from defending the gruesomeness which was practised at the time through those courts, only we want to note that the human, when once his zeal for something is inflamed, soon does not recognise the boundaries anymore and goes much further than the achieving of the goal demands. This experience is confirmed through all the centuries, and I believe our time does not form any exception to it.

It is indeed not the intention to shine a light on the Inquisition or draw sacrifices from its claws; we have merely cited it in order to characterise to some extent the time which we are planning to survey, and at the same time to show the narrowness of the path to which the researcher is restricted.

Everywhere is spirit. At all times it has made itself known. Indeed, the experience has been made that it is often easier to obtain on the narrow path than on the great highway where you often do not see the truth, being dazzled by will o' the wisps and artificial stars.

I do not want to speak further here in order to not come in hostile contact with the world's wise men; but the following judgement I believe to be permitted to express without timidity: unity of belief would be a great fortune for humanity; but still greater advantage would arise if on every path a sufficient number of enlightened people were to stand who, being instructed by the spirit, were capable of showing the wandering ones the true goal of their journey.

We have found in the thirteenth century such a guide who appeared as a teacher, and we want to use his hints so that we, like his students, attain the goal of our life.

***

The Family Er..k..ng

In that time when blindness reigned, when the Christian religion had indeed already spread over all of Germany, but had merged with such orthodox, in part even heathen concepts that it was often difficult for the adherents to distinguish the true from the false, the knight Sigismund von Er..k..ng lived, and had marked his banner, for a sign of his faith, with the cross. He was the father of three sons whom he raised for the continuation of his career and who were instructed in all the virtues which befitted a Christian knight.

His two eldest sons, Sigismund and Bernhard, he had already granted the knight's sword and called upon them to never avoid a fight where it concerned God and fatherland.

Opportunity soon showed itself for responding to this request. The French, arch enemies of Germany who were incessantly endeavouring to set the German imperial crown on the head of their rulers, had crossed the borders and penetrated through the Black Forest and Odenwald in order to annex it.

Er..k..ng, member of the German knighthood, had sworn never to allow the imperial dignity to be granted to a foreigner so long as he could still wield his sword. Hence he took the field at the head of his mercenary cavalry with his two eldest, and summoned all the valiant German knights to join with him.

His youngest son, Gottfried, how was barely fifteen years old, he left to look after his mother, and at the same time gave the warden of the castle the order to instruct him in all the chivalric sports and form out of him an effective warrior.

Mathilde — that was the name of his wife — who had to part from her sons for the first time, poured bitter tears and asked them to take care of their lives and not plunge her into grief and sorrow; but called upon the father to guard over them and lead them safely with his experience.

The departure was stirring. They all promised the mother to return again because God would protect them in every danger.

The procession moved out. The abandoned mother went tearfully to her chamber in order to give free rein to her anguish and to plead to heaven for those drawing away.

The struggle lasted a long time, for the enemy was strong and brave and defended every foot of land which he had to abandon again for life and death.

A year passed and Mathilde still waited in vain for news from the field or the return of her family.

In Germany parties had formed on account of the choice of emperor which stood hostile towards one another, lands and roads were made unsafe and thereby made difficult any news from those distant. Warlike hordes even passed through Er..k..ng's domains and committed oppressions as if they were in enemy lands. In the castle itself Mathilde did not seem safe anymore, for already she had been twice called upon to give it up and to allow it to be possessed as a security for the future emperor.

Mathilde rejected every demand and commanded the castle warden to take every measure for the most dogged defence. She infused her soldiers with courage herself and had the castle gate closed day and night in order to not be surprised by a sudden attack.

Often she went down on her knees before God in her chamber, prayed for protection or news of her husband and her sons, and of aid for herself; but she did not find anymore the consolation she had formerly felt. "It was better previously," she then said full of sadness; "then fairies and spirits of the ancestors came to the abandoned women, gave them advice, and brought news of those distant. Now I plead in vain; no hope illuminates me, and no power from eternity hears and strengthens me in my misfortune."

Finally one day around midnight a messenger came to the gates and desired entry. He had crept through forests and swamps in order to reach the castle. The castle warden

The Family Er..k..ng

questioned him and found his mission confirmed. "What do you bring?", he asked.

Messenger: "News for the lady of the castle."

Warden: "Is it good?"

Messenger: "Oh, no! The enemy becomes ever more and our side ever less. One knight after the other leaves in order to look after themselves at home, and those left behind fall under the blows of the superior numbers."

Warden: "How is it going for our own?"

Messenger: "Badly. They desire to go home because there is no honour to be won there anymore."

Warden: "And our noble knight and his sons?"

Messenger: "The knight remains true to his vow to defend the German imperial crown against every foreigner. 'May they also be divided amongst themselves,' he says; 'it will balance out; but if a foreigner lifts himself onto our throne, then Germany's honour is gone for eternity.'"

Warden: "If in Germany there were many such men of integrity, then it would be different. But his sons?"

Messenger: "Are like him; only a pity that the elder one, Sigismund, is already departed. He found his death with an ambush where he had to battle with a small group against an enemy six times as strong."

The castle warden became hot of heart when he heard this news. "Oh, the poor noble woman! How this news will shake her!"

Mathilde was not yet in bed. She was abandoning herself alone to the presentiments of her heart, which were not announcing anything good. "I am feeling so anxious," she thought; "as if a great misfortune were close to me." She now heard the knocking at the castle gate, heard voices talking, and sent someone down to learn what was happening.

"Let the lady of the castle sleep in peace", the castle warden said; "tomorrow there will be time enough for bad news." Only Mathilde wanted to know everything that day, and called the castle warden and the messenger to herself.

The news hit her hard. No tears came to her eyes to give her relief. She dismissed those present with few words and surrendered herself to a dull brooding. "Fate is afflicting me terribly", she said; "and I must not grumble, that is what religion teaches me. Good, it is! I want to endure and wait. But it must not remain so! I do not want to wear my existence in constant uncertainty, like a burden which you would rather be rid of. I must have certainty for the future, otherwise I suspect my faith in God and eternity will have flown and my situation will become even more terrible."

The next morning she called the castle chaplain to her and entered into the following conversation with him.

Lady: "You have heard what misfortune has struck me?"

Chaplain: "Yes."

Lady: "Can you grant me solace?"

Chaplain: "Not with certainty."

Lady: "Has the religion no remedies for wounds to the heart?"

Chaplain: "Oh yes. But they need time."

Lady: "Has it no remedies for averting misfortune that has not yet happened?"

Chaplain: "Yes."

Lady: "Which?"

Chaplain: "Child-like trust."

Lady: "I had trust and what are the fruits of it?"

Chaplain: "I lament for you, noble lady. Your loss is great, but the religion does not belong to what it does not touch. The workings of heaven are miraculous, and nobody can fathom the counsel of heaven."

Mathilde raised her eyes at these last words to heaven and said deeply moved, "God! Forgive me if I despair; forgive me if I am resolved to break through the night in which my soul languishes. Nobody, they say, can fathom your counsel, and formerly it was though obvious to mortals. The patriarchs, so I was taught, walked in God and were the servants of his will. Abraham foresaw his own and the fate of his family. Joshua, Gideon, and David were warriors to whom the almighty lent power, protection, and victory. Even my ancestors had through spiritual influence the fate of their own in their power and were not a victim of the martyring uncertainty as we are in our days. Is that consequence of a better religion or consequence of our weakness? Reverend!", she continued, turning to the chaplain; "give me information about that so that I know what I have to hope for."

The chaplain avoided her gaze in dismay. He had indeed heard the question, but did not possess the courage to enter into its sense, and finally told the noble lady she should not tempt God, and not brood over things which are hidden from us for our happiness.

Lady: "Much is hidden, it is true; but for our happiness you claim! I deny it. Darkness is the greatest evil, but light awakes entire nature to life. Our religion, according to your own testimony, desires no darkness, but rather it should become day in us through it. I have this belief, I hope to die in this belief, and hence I called you to me to ask you to give my youngest son instruction in that power of belief in which the aforementioned warriors won victory, and which is in a position to move mountains."

Chaplain: "I understand you. It is no bold thought which I cannot rebuke, but also cannot approve. Forgive me, noble lady, if I seek to divert you from your intention. I consider child-like piety and surrender to be the ornaments of religion. Misfortune and trouble are on earth, it is truth; we have much to endure and to bear, but the prospect is given to us that after a short time of testing all storms abate, all that is lost is found, and all worries and laments are repaid with eternal joy."

Lady: "This doctrine is pious and mild like your heart. Formerly it was dear to me, and I found refreshment in it; only now it does not console me anymore, and hence I hope and expect from you the fulfillment of my wish."

Chaplain: "You are insisting on it. Noble lady! I regret to have to explain to you that I am too weak to provide such instruction. But, in order to give you proof of my respect for your house and to justify the honour of our sublime religion in your eyes, I will make my way and seek a teacher for your son who is up to such a task."

The noble lady was moved by the good-heartedness of the chaplain. "You are giving me a ray of hope", she said. "I recognise the greatness of your sacrifice in taking yourself on a journey during these unrests; but count on the thanks of the mother who can only achieve reassurance in this way."

The chaplain took his leave and was leaving the castle already on the next day. The noble lady gifted him amply, and asked him to return again and close out his days there.

***

The New Chaplain

Four weeks after the departure of the chaplain a stranger appeared at the castle gates and desired entry in his name. The noble lady immediately let him enter, refreshed him with drink and food, and invited him up to her chamber.

After short greetings she inquired after his name, his former residence, and all the circumstances which she considered necessary to know about the person of her future chaplain on which to some extent the fate of her house rested.

"I am Joseph K..i..l," the clergyman began; "the village of T..r in Lorraine is my place of birth. My parents were rich, but god-fearing and devoted to the teachings of religion. I was the eldest son of four and, because I showed a talent for learning and liked visiting the church, I was intended for the clergy. All which was required for this goal was amply spent on me, and my parents celebrated the day as their happiest on which I read my first mass in my place of birth. Now I was a priest, was rich, and had the prospect of the most brilliant career which can be achieved in my class; but through the desired knowledge my life took on a different shape, and I foresaw clearly that it would not suffice for me if I could win from it a different view.

Because I was not required to immediately accept any post which was offered to me, I asked my parents to let me travel so that I would find the opportunity to investigate the spirit of Christianity in its fullest depths and to learn to exercise the duties of a clergyman in their entirety. They gave their consent and my father offered a significant sum for this aim. Italy was the goal of my journey; there, as it were in the cradle of Christianity, I hoped to satisfy all my expectations, but I noticed with astonishment that not everything was just as I imagined.

I travelled from town to town and arrived finally at the centre of the world, at the acclaimed Rome, and submitted there the recommendations which I had received in Rheims and Strasbourg, and my astonishment grew when I saw the priesthood occupied more with worldly than with spiritual things.

I had been living in Rome already for half a year and had already given up hope of finding some grounds for my wish for higher knowledge, when I was called to Cardinal C...h. He received me obligingly, and asked after a short introduction, 'You have already been in Rome a long time?'

Me: 'Half a year.'

Cardinal: 'And the goal of your being here?'

Me: 'Pure knowledge in the doctrine of Christianity.'

Cardinal: 'Have you found what you sought?'

I was apprehensive about answering it and hence became embarrassed. He noticed that and said, 'Honesty is indeed not required everywhere, but here it would be certainly in its place.'

Me: 'I could be mistaken, but I have not found it as I had expected it.'

Cardinal: 'In what way have you found your expectations deceived in the main?'

Me: 'Because I saw the priesthood occupied more with worldly than with spiritual things.'

Cardinal: 'You speak like every layperson who wants to separate the spirit from the world. Spirit and world are contained in one another, body and spirit condition one another, for without spirit the human body cannot exist and without body the spirit cannot reveal itself. Have you understood me?'

Me: 'I want to consider it and seek to clarify it.'

Cardinal: 'You have talents and, so it seems, courage and zeal. Visit me again.'

Strangers were announced and I gave my leave with the question, 'When can I again have the fortune of seeing you?' — 'Every day', he said; 'if you want. I must examine you and seek what is to be brought out from you.'

I made use of his permission and visited him almost every day for seven years. It would be long-winded to repeat here

The New Chaplain

everything which he spoke of with me and in what way he opened my innermost being; enough, in him I had found what I never suspected, a man in spirit, a researcher and thinker to whom the secrets of our sublime religion had been revealed and had stamped him as a true priest of God.

After seven years I felt capable of acting alone, and asked him therefore to obtain the permission of the Holy Father to go into the world and to promulgate the spirit of true Christianity amongst the people. My request was granted and with some emotion I took leave of the Cardinal, who was to me father, guide, and everything in that he had drawn me out of the darkness and lit in me the light of life.

Before I left him, he gave me the following lesson.

'If you want to be useful to the church, then wander carefully.

You have fathomed the secrets of religion, but you are still not entirely mature, for you lack experience. Do not give away anything which you do not fully possess.

If you want to teach, then test your audience for what they can bear; for many a small light is more bearable than a large one which blinds their eyes.

The first laws of our religion are love for God and for the neighbour; to spread this you do not need any limits, for you cannot do much in this.

It is more difficult to show humans the source of knowledge which is contained in the holy books. Falsely understood wisdom leads easily to the darkness of smugness where you forget the boundary which separates the divine from the worldly.

The power of belief which the Gospels teach us is the most dangerous cliff on which you can lead the audience. The human, if he once recognises those powers which are invincible and work victoriously, easily loses himself, forgets the light which gives him the strength, becomes a monster, a criminal, and instead of heaven serves hell and his own arrogance.'"

Mathilde had listened to this tale with special attention and responded, "I can easily guess why you shared so fully with me the rule of behaviour which you received. It is not time now to give me your view on it; when you have recovered from your journey we want to speak more about this subject. But I must confess as much to you, that I thank God for leading you here; for in you I believe I have found the man who can fulfill my wish and reassure me."

She remained alone and considered what she had heard. "Love", she said; "is a sublime commandment which could raise us to paradise if our hearts were not wounded so often. To prevent these wounds cannot be a sin if we do it in the power of that which comes from the universal and which is indeed itself eternal love."

Mathilde called the chaplain to her the next day in order to discuss with him the manner, as well as the time when he wanted to begin his instruction. He seemed apprehensive and made the attempt to divert her from her intention, only she interrupted him and said, "If you can teach me that hearts do not bleed more when they are wounded, then I will honour your suggestion, if you are incapable of this, then I ask you to begin the instruction with my son."

Chaplain: "It will be, I will dare it; I want to examine his powers and, if I consider him to be capable, will show him the way to a life course which leads him to the highest goal of existence."

Mathilde felt strengthened by the received hope; but he asked for wisdom so that his work would succeed and not lead to misfortune.

***

Gottfried von Er..k..ng

It is proper that we get somewhat more closely acquainted with that one of whom so much is spoken and who in the course of this story is the main character.

Gottfried was, as was already noted above, the youngest son of the knightly house of Er..k..ng. Although nine years younger than Bernhard, he had already practised in chivalric sport with his two brothers, and, when they mounted their great battle steeds, he sat on a nag of such a smaller sort that he stood in great disparity with the others. The servants of the castle indeed laughed over this little knight and over his little steed, but that did not worry him, he swung his little lance and his light sword with a zeal as though it were about life and death. His mother saw this play and was often scared of heart when she considered that it would transform itself in a few years into bloody earnest.

Already at the time the resolve was germinating in her which she was now in a position to perform in concept; to educate him to be a warrior who was raised above every danger, bore his fate in his hands, and was not subject to blind chance. She made thousands of plans to put her intention to work, only she failed every time on the disbelief of those with whom she shared her intention, because they considered such a goal to be impossible. She would probably also have given it up had not the war and the death of her elder son led her to it anew.

But now her intention was irrevocably fixed, and in order to realise it she was turning to the chaplain.

Gottfried knew of the plan of his mother and would have long since agreed to put it into practice, but it was for him like with her; the matter was considered to be a daydream and he was sent off in that way.

Irregardless of this he was not at ease. The idea of an invincible knight had struck root in him at some point, and he often thought of whether it would not be possible to arrive on the trail of the matter alone.

He had heard many stories of gnomes and fairies who lent mortals protection and supernatural powers; the stories of Biblical heroes were just as remarkable to him and he often found himself tempted to believe that it only came down to the person themselves to acquire all these genies, angels, and supernatural powers.

He discussed this often with his mother, but she, as much as she also wished it, did not know of any means to name for obtaining such characteristics.

A old squire whom Gottfried's father had liked to have around him and who accompanied him on all his campaigns finally became his close friend, and he gave him a few hints which confirmed for him the matter and increased his thirst for knowledge of secret powers.

He made various attempts to put a few of the given rules into use, but the matter was a failure and he ended up in new embarrassment. The idea of miraculous powers had passed over into his entire being, and it hurt him deeply that he also could not obtain any certainty anywhere.

The squire indeed remained true to his claim that not everyone could use the key, or as he suggested, the handle with success if he had not previously made himself competent; but in what this competence consisted, he could not or did not want to say.

Gottfried had stood at the point of breaking with him if the going on campaign had not separated them without this. Now he was left alone, and brooded to himself over fairies, mermaids, and gnomes, and could often not comprehend why none of these beings rewarded his belief and showed themselves to him.

He was in this mood when the new chaplain arrived at the castle. Because he knew from his mother the goal for which the chaplain had been called, he looked at him as a sort of wondrous phenomenon, and could barely wait to come into contact with him, his future teacher.

Finally the yearned-for day arrived. His mother had it said to him that the chaplain wished to speak to him in the morning in order to make known to him the future plan of instruction. He could barely wait out the time, and got up very early the next day in order to be in readiness if that man were to have him called or should in any case come to him. Neither thing happened, but instead they met in the courtyard of the castle and began the instruction.

***

The Instruction

Gottfried, as much as he also felt he was the son of the house whom you must treat with a certain degree of reverence, was embarrassed though when the chaplain spoke to him. He did not know right away of anything suitable to respond with and said, "Welcome here, chaplain!"

Chaplain: "Accept my greetings, noble lord."

Gottfried: "You will be staying with us for a long time?"

Chaplain: "That depends on you."

Gottfried: "On me?"

Chaplain: "I am supposed to be instructing you in the art of living."

Gottfried: "Mother told me about that."

Chaplain: "This art you learn though only through courage and solidity, for many obstacles are to be conquered and hard struggles to be overcome."

Gottfried: "I can be persistent and give you my word that no struggle scares me if I know that I will arrive at the goal."

Chaplain: "Then it would be a pity to tarry and not begin the instruction immediately. Good! Then listen. The first thing is to know yourself. You are a brave knight's son, have grown up as a noble, the lordly sense has been deeply rooted in you. All that must change. The human alone can obtain true power, for he is the one who has risen from the power and can develop it in himself. Do you understand me?"

Gottfried: "I suspect what you want to say, but I cannot yet clearly grasp it. Hence allow me to ask, what difference is there between the human and the noble?"

Chaplain: "A parrot says what you teach it, the human does not need teaching."

Gottfried: "So the poor people are better off than we are, for in their hearts no noble sense lies hidden."

Chaplain: "The mind of the servant oppresses them."
Gottfried: "Accordingly there would be few true humans?"
Chaplain: "Very few."
Gottfried: "That is strange though. Indeed it is now clear to me, but my heart bristles against it."
Chaplain: "It is a good sign if you are clearly and distinctly conscious of this feeling. We want to build our instruction on this feeling and seek the new humans hand in hand. Enough for today."

They parted. The chaplain went to his room in order to himself live, the noble, however, walked up and down the courtyard for a long time pondering and put effort into making the words of his teacher properly understandable.

The next day he came to the chaplain again and said, "I have thought about your words and find that they are clever, only it will be difficult to separate the one from the other, for I have found that, even if I do not want to, I always think and act as a noble."

Chaplain: "That is good. Anyone who has once found the one can also discover the other. Only bravely forwards!"

Gottfried: "If I now ask, why does the human always get caught in his clothes? That is, why is his class so important to him? So the natural answer is because he is educated for it. That seems according to your words a mistake, and hence would it be better if the human had no education at all?"

Chaplain: "It would at least not be as bad at all as you think. But now we must not yet get mixed up in that; a time will come when it will be clear to you that the first human, who also had no education, was no worse than we are. But until you have arrived at this knowledge we must still have a little patience, and hence I ask you, what must the human do?"

Gottfried: "Good."
Chaplain: "What is good?"
Gottfried: "Everything which is right?"
Chaplain: "What is right?"
Gottfried: "Everything which must be."
Chaplain: "That is well answered. I could indeed ask, what is that which must be? And there you would falter in your

answer, for to do what must be is the first and last law of God and of nature."

Gottfried: "Is it possible?! Explain this to me through an example."

Chaplain: "A carter is supposed to take stones to a high-placed castle. The way is bad, and only with effort could you travel it. The carter, however, offers to deliver the stones. He harnesses his wagon with as many draught animals as he considers necessary, and drives the loaded wagon up it. The carter had done what he had to do in order to fulfill his promise."

Gottfried: "That is true, but I cannot find the application."

Chaplain: "This is easy when we consider that the human must also go up into the heights, although he has a great load to bear."

Gottfried: "What are the heights which you mean?"

Chaplain: "Life in its purest light."

Gottfried: "What is the load?"

Chaplain: "We ourselves; our ego."

Gottfried: "And the draught animals?"

Chaplain: "Our life's desires."

Gottfried: "What? And these should be of assistance to bringing us into the heights?"

Chaplain: "Who else then? Have you other powers which can draw you? Have you other means? No! What we possess we must learn to use; what we do not yet have, and even if it were the best, has no power for us, is not present for us."

Gottfried: "You are making me confused. From youth on I was taught you must muffle the desires, suppress and even eliminate them. But you are teaching me the opposite. How shall I help myself then?"

Chaplain: "You must be modest, that is, you must set yourself only one goal, but not several! Then seek the desires which incline towards that goal, give yourself over to them, and you will see how easily it will go."

Gottfried: "Then indeed the task of achieving a high goal is not difficult if our nature itself draws us to it."

Chaplain: "So it is. The matter itself is not difficult, but the struggle to mediate the desires, to select those which should be active, and to bring the others to rest, that is difficult, that is a struggle which only the clever and brave fighter succeeds at."

Gottfried: "I comprehend it. I want now to also set an example: when I plan to fulfill the wish of someone who was otherwise disagreeable to me, I must forget his offensiveness and only consider his good characteristics. I am then drawn by these and fulfill my intention with light effort."

Chaplain: "You have spoken well. Meditate on this and tomorrow more on it."

It would be going too far to set down all the conversations of the chaplain and his student here. It is enough if we say that Gottfried in a period of two years quite understood him and recognised the clear signs of the natural human in himself.

In this year the castle had not altered much; the knight and his son still stood in the field and battled under great strain with alternating fortune. The unrest in Germany was getting the upper hand more and more, and you did not know in the end anymore which party you actually belonged to. Luxembourg had a great following; Austria no less a one, and Bavaria, which lay in the middle of all these struggles, thereby achieved superiority because it always obtained the lead through its proximity. In this state of things Mathilde did not yet have any hope of soon seeing her son and husband again. Even if they had made the decision to return home, they saw themselves cut off by the Bavarians who had struck up their victorious banner in that region.

Mathilde, informed of all of this, saw the impossibility of giving and receiving news, and consoled herself with the prospect that her younger son would one day part the clouds which were veiling her future.

Gottfried exercised in the chivalric sports alongside the instruction which he enjoyed with the chaplain, and everybody looked with astonishment at his agility and strength.

The chaplain, who guided these exercises, even if invisibly, brought to his student's attention the inner powers of the human, how they often slumbered, then stepped forth at once and gave us agility, courage, and acumen.

"It is true!", Gottfried said, "sometimes you perform something which the moment before seemed impossible to us. So

The Instruction

it is too with our thoughts — you can brood over a topic for days, but you are as if stuck, and suddenly it stands clearly before us. From where does it come about that this often goes so slowly?"

Chaplain: "Because we make detours."

Gottfried: "Detours? That I do not comprehend."

Chaplain: "But it is so."

Gottfried: "Explain it to me."

Chaplain: "If you want to speak to someone and you do not know where he lives, then you must first search for him. Is that not true?"

Gottfried: "Understood."

Chaplain: "So it is with our powers — if we knew where the powers were seated, then we could quickly call them forth. Thus too with thoughts. If we knew the seat of thought, then it would cost us no effort to receive thoughts from it which enlightened us over anything which is hidden from us."

Gottfried: "That is good. Now the question is how do you learn to recognise the seat of these powers?"

Chaplain: "Quite right. Anyone who solves this question has attained the goal. But, in order not to mix up one thing with the other, we want to first examine thought in order to get to know the path to it."

Gottfried: "I am full of expectation."

Chaplain: "A principle exists here which is stated in the following way: any power can only think itself or that which agrees with it."

Gottfried: "That would be strange."

Chaplain: "It is in keeping with nature. The ear can do nothing else but think powers of the ear; it cannot imagine any colours, measure any surfaces, in short, nothing which does not belong to its sphere. When we speak of smell, the nose is thinking; and only the palate alone can judge the tastefulness of food."

Gottfried: "It is true, I have made the attempt while you were speaking. It is absolutely true! But where does this lead to?"

Chaplain: "As far as the power of the human reaches. As far as he is in a position to think and to feel. In the endlessness, in the highest of all, in the innermost of all nature and his own being."

Gottfried: "Give me yet a rule, or better, let me make another attempt."

Chaplain: "Well now, with what do you think of your mother?"

Gottfried: "With my heart."

Chaplain: "With what do you think of her figure?"

Gottfried: "With my eyes."

Chaplain: "With what do you think of the sound of her voice?"

Gottfried: "With my ears."

Chaplain: "But when you think of her as your mother, as your carer, as your guide and nurse, then you think her with your heart. And the more thankfulness and love you imagine these characteristics with, the deeper is the thought, which we describe, however, with the expression feelings because we feel it in the heart."

Gottfried: "Thank you. You have given me information which instructs me about many things. I will exercise myself in the analysis of these powers of thought, and hope to find out for myself in the end where the strength of the warrior resides when he takes the field for oppressed innocents, for his fatherland, for God and honour."

Chaplain: "Your hand, young man! I see you will go far."

The next day Gottfried came very delighted to the chaplain and said, "I have discovered a lot. I know the power of the rider, of the warrior with the spear and with the sword, I also feel already how the shield rises. Oh, dear chaplain, God has sent you to me! Guide me only forwards and do not forget to teach me more and more what is good and right, for I have already found a few times that one often does not like to do what must be."

Chaplain: "Welcome, noble lord! You are diligent, as I hear, which pleases me. To make attempts by yourself testifies to zeal, and that is praiseworthy. Only we must not forget that you must first learn to stand before you can run and fight. Do not misunderstand me though! I am not rebuking what you have done, I am only making you attentive so that, in order to climb the ladder safely, you step on the

The Instruction

lowest rung first, then continue, one after the other. Is it not so?"

Gottfried: "Who can deny it? Lead me to the ladder."

Chaplain: "We must first place it."

Gottfried: "Place it?"

Chaplain: "Yes. It is still hanging askew in a dark barn."

Gottfried: "Then show it to me."

Chaplain: "You are it."

Gottfried: "Explain it to me."

Chaplain: "Tell me, when you think, where do you thoughts begin to stir?"

Gottfried: "In my head surely."

Chaplain: "In the head or on the head?"

Gottfried: "That I do not know."

Chaplain: "When you know that, then you have the ladder and can attempt to place it. Farewell until tomorrow."

The next day Gottfried arrived highly discontented with himself. "I have sought", he said to the chaplain, "the entire day and almost the entire night, and am incapable of completing the task. At first you said each power can only think itself, or what agrees with itself, but now you ask where the thought begins to stir? It is thus a new question and cannot be answered in the above way."

Chaplain: "Quite right. At first you see, hear, and feel an object or imagine it yourself. But now this seen or imagined thing comes into action, becomes ours and we think about it. With what does this happen at first?"

Gottfried: "I do not know."

Chaplain: "What are the aids to thinking?"

Gottfried: "Words."

Chaplain: "Where do these form?"

Gottfried: "In the mouth."

Chaplain: "So it is. In the mouth the thought opens its activity and only then goes on the destined path again back to that power which produced it or agreed with it."

Gottfried: "Give me an example."

Chaplain: "The miller takes the grain from the sack, shakes it on the mill, makes flour from it, and fills the sack anew with it."

Gottfried: "I cannot find the application."

Chaplain: "The mind has received an idea, now it gives it by means of speech to the mouth, this lets it go through the body in order to crush it, then it comes back into the mind as perfected thought."

Gottfried: "The doctrine is clear, but the practice?"

Chaplain: "Is subject to a few difficulties. But practice conquers everything."

Gottfried: "Thank you. I will certainly not be inactive."

Chaplain: "One more thing. Do not forget the ladder!"

Gottfried: "Does this belong to the matter?"

Chaplain: "Very much so. When the mouth begins its activity, then it all comes down to that we observe the appropriate ladder. First you must place the ladder on the ground and then begin the activity."

Gottfried: "Teach me that!"

Chaplain: "So listen. The human stands in his feet, if these are not steady, then he easily falls. Examine that and the come back."

Gottfried was in a desperate situation. Learning to think in his feet did not work in his mind. He made every possible attempt, but he despaired a number of times almost of ever succeeding. But finally he succeeded in it, and after five weeks he came back and said, "Forgive me that I hesitated so long this time, but the matter was all too difficult for me. But all at once I found it."

Chaplain: "Listen further. The feet are the first rung, from these you climb to the knees, then to the hips, to the navel and the solar plexus, to the neck, and finally to the head. The ladder is erected, now learn to climb further."

Gottfried had to take an entire year to fulfill this task. He indeed visited the chaplain daily, but received no teaching from him, instead they discussed the dignity and the powers of the human in general. But finally the student thought he stood at the top of the ladder and said, "Test me for whether I have achieved it." — "You have achieved it;" the chaplain replied, "but a skilled climber also grasps about himself with his hands, that will be easy for you, I think. More difficult, however, is what I will yet say: everything which we want to accomplish externally must also happen internally. The first climbing touches only the skin, now we want to penetrate

The Instruction

through the flesh, through the bones, through kidneys, liver, lungs, and heart, even through the marrow of the bones, in order to approach the desired perfection."

Now the struggles began. Fire, cold, every evil showed itself in the body of the student so that he would have been defeated without the encouragement of his teacher, and would not have achieved the victory of the cross which the chaplain placed before his eyes as a gleaming goal. But finally the storms abated within him and he stood there as a new man.

"Now let us form the warrior;" the chaplain said. "The feet stand, the hands are lively, the entire body has developed to free activity and received the spirit. Now forwards! Do not waver, whatever you meet and whatever faces show themselves to you; it is the inner human who now feels and strives to reveal his characteristics.

The bold climber does not always need ever rung, he often leaps over one, two, three, sometimes even five, in order to arrive quicker in the heights. He frees himself from all bonds and flies up with the power of the eagle.

The language forms in the mouth; only it must penetrate us everywhere so that our entire nature becomes the language in which the word of God sounds and shows us the truth. Obey this word when you hear it, undertake nothing without its counsel, and a new day will dawn in you.

The inner eye must see, the inner ear must hear, and all the senses must find themselves in the inner-being, in their root, then the human has arisen to life and the crucifixion is behind him.

You now know the powers, but what they are capable of working, only belief can teach. It is not to be fathomed and nobody has entirely accomplished it yet. The eternal says, 'Are you too afraid of me to believe or of thinking me too great? Look on the myriads of stars, I have placed them there in order to illuminate those who approach me. Look at the arch of the heavens in the most beautiful blue, I created that vault in order to give a temple to those who pray to me. Anyone who prays to me in the spirit, I hear and the compliance already lies in the request. Anyone who speaks to me in my language speaks in me and everything which is mine is his.' More I may not say, you know now everything, and what you need you must obtain through yourself."

The instruction was now at an end and the chaplain called upon Gottfried, who was now twenty three years old, to practise and to prepare, because soon the hour would come to take the test of whether he did not need the school any further.

Gottfried squeezed the chaplain's hand warmly and replied, "I cannot express what I feel for you. You have torn me from the night of living death and called me forth to a higher existence. The power which guided you and which you awakened in me shall reward you; I can only thank and love you."

Chaplain: "Love is the only reward which can become mine and delight me. Hence do not forget me when your life course has once begun and you do not see me anymore. Our hearts shall stay embraced amidst all the changes of time."

Gottfried sank with emotion onto his chest and said, "Eternal love!" — "Eternal love!", the chaplain replied and pulled him, like father to son, to his chest.

***

Germany

In public matters much had changed. The pretenders to the imperial throne acted militantly towards one another and put the German knighthood in the most painful uncertainty. Nobody knew which party to take up because you could not know the outcome in advance. Neutrality was impossible, however, and so the smaller ones sought to combine amongst themselves in order to tip the scales somewhere. Such a plan though progressed very slowly and the poor fatherland saw itself as the scene of devastating wars.

The French had been pushed back in the meantime and seemed to abandon their intentions on the German imperial dignity, but the struggle with them had cost many victims, for the core of the knighthood lay partly heavily wounded or had remained on the battlefield. Amongst the latter was also found Bernhard, the second son of the knight Er..k..ng; he himself, however, saw no hope of undertaking anything for the benefit of the fatherland.

He would have long since gone home, but he did not want to expose himself to the necessity of having to declare for a party, and hence he found it more advisable to remain for the moment in Lorraine as a guard against the French in order to hinder them from making use of the disunity of the Germans.

Mathilde received news of him and of the death of her second son. "I am destined to endure loss!", she said. "Good for us that I raised a support for myself in my youngest son who will not break so easily."

She grieved deeply, but pulled herself together because she had foreseen as it were that this blow would yet come. She now feared still for her husband and wished longingly to at least see him one more time before death parted them forever.

Thus the matter stood when the chaplain declared his student to be ready to have an effect in public life.

The expectations which harboured for him were various. Many thought he would seek settle the public matters as a learned judge through disputations. Others harboured little trust in him because he was too young and had occupied himself in recent times more with the chaplain than with the weapons. The lady of the castle, however, could barely wait for the time of his public activity and encouraged him at every opportunity to make himself competent for it.

The chaplain observed his student in silence, let him now freely do as he liked when he inspected the soldiers and gave them rules of conduct.

He saw him romping about with his battle steed and swinging his lance. When he had dismounted from the horse, the chaplain said, "I fear it goes for me like with the goddess Thetis who, because she forgot when bathing her son Achilles in the Lethe to also wet his heels, thereby made him vulnerable. — We have forgotten the fist which with you is not yet lively and not fortified." Gottfried thanked him, went away, and in five days he said to him, "In my fist is powerful life."

***

Gottfried's First Deed

A large mob of soldiers, led by the brave knight B...ng, arrived before the castle and desired entry in the name of the Duke of Luxembourg. Gottfried heard this request and said, "I do not know the Duke."

The knight B...ng, whom this answer irritated, made it clear to him that if he did not hand over the castle in twenty four hours then he would storm it and destroy the nest.

"Tell the knight", Gottfried said; "that I will not hand over the castle in twenty four hours, nor ever, and if this answer does not please him then I will come down to him and show him that the power of men still flows in our bones."

B...ng straightaway let preparations be made for an attack and moved so close to the walls of the castle that the besiegers and the besieged could converse with some effort. Gottfried saw these movements and stood calmly at his vantage point. B...ng called to him, "Come down boy, if you are brave enough!" Gottfried responded, "Just collect your people in the meantime so that I receive something to do."

Thus they mocked each other for a long time. Soon the soldiers were also taking part and increased their lust for battle to the highest degree. Finally Gottfried left the wall and said to himself, "Now it is time, the stars are twinkling, that is a sign of victory. It will happen like the spirit showed me."

He had the gate opened and went down from the castle with his small group. When the besiegers saw them, such a tiny number, they erupted in a loud laughter and found it barely worth the trouble to set themselves in order.

"The wing flies and rises!", Gottfried cried. "Up, now to the enemy!"

As quickly as the wind drives through trees that have shed their leaves, they broke through the line of the enemy and spread terror through them. B...ng, before he knew what had happened, was disarmed by Gottfried and knocked from his horse. The battle was quickly at an end; the enemy surrendered and asked to be allowed to leave in return for the hostages they offered.

Gottfried was content with that. "Leave", he said; "and do not come back, otherwise I cannot protect you anymore, for a warrior is with me to whom all enemies are only dust in a strong wind." When the prisoners wanted to draw lots for the hostages, he said, "I do not need them; in my inner-being and in my breast lies a guarantee for me which surpasses all which humans can give."

He drew back into the castle with his men. Everybody had gathered at the gate to greet the victors. Mathilde was at their head and poured out tears of joy when her son dismounted from his battle steed and hurried to her. "God alone", she cried out, "is in a position to return the delight which I now feel!" — The procession now slowly moved on, and when they had drawn up in the castle courtyard, the little bell in the castle chapel was tolled on the orders of the chaplain in order to assemble the residents and to spur them on to thank God fervently for rescuing them from this danger.

When the chaplain and Gottfried found themselves alone together, the former said solemnly, "A third one is missing here for us to form a circle. Only in a circle can you celebrate an occasion. A celebration, however, must be enjoyed after every first deed which a mortal accomplishes in the spirit. Good, the spirit shall be the third one here, and so we want to rejoice that God so wonderfully and lovingly devotes himself to the human who seeks to recognise him in the spirit. It is a feast day today which shall unite us with him in a bond of blessing, for all who are around us, for all who plead for help, for all who trust in God, indeed for all who languish in misery and dare not raise their voice from fright and fear of people.

Now choose, stern knight, for the sign of your loyalty, in this circle your own symbol for your escutcheon, a symbol which lives in you and which comes from the spirit and can transport you into it at any moment."

Gottfried's First Deed

Gottfried thought to himself for a few moments and said, "My escutcheon and my banner is: 'CREDO!' This word, intertwined in such a form as

$$\maltese$$

shall be my escutcheon and adorn my coat of arms, and propagate to my distant offspring."

The chaplain offered him his hand and said, "The day is ordained! It is the day of your refound life and will be celebrated by you with great joy whenever it returns each year."

"So be it!", Gottfried responded.

They went now each to his own tasks which the mood of the heart or their calling prescribed for them.

Only after the accomplished deed was Gottfried capable of recognising the standpoint on which his attained powers placed him. He dedicated himself therefore still more seriously to the knowledge of his inner life, and finally brought it to the point that he felt his ego in its innermost of all places, from where he saw the hosts of eternity, broke through the night of the future, and looked on his deeds in advance. "How great is God!", he said in such moments; "and how necessary it is to feel and to recognise him in yourself."

***

New Enemies

In Prussia, which at that time still found itself in a rough state, a branch of the Livonian order of the Brothers of the Sword settled, built and conquered castles, and sought to spread its power across Germany too.

The Duke of Brandenburg, although not a member, was assisting their intentions in order to keep a counterweight against the German emperors in case they strove to increase their power. Thereby encouraged, they now attacked one German knight after the other, and when they succeeded in conquering a castle, they considered it to be their legal property.

Gottfried heard of these incursions and violent acts, and was quickly resolved to put an end to them; only he had to first take precautions for the security of his own possessions. To this end he undertook a foray through the region and ejected everybody who did not avow peace.

Now he made his way towards the aforementioned Prussian knights. They had penetrated over the Elbe and many castles and fortresses had surrendered to them for fear of cruel mistreatment. Gottfried appeared with a small handful of men, called the neighbouring German knights together and said, "I am here to liberate Germany from the shameful attacks and oppressions of a number of knights who have the intention of enriching themselves with our property and bringing us in the end under their dominion. Anyone who is resolved to stand by me, follow me!"

The knights heard this suggestion, but could not come to any decision when they considered his small war group, and advised him to first make an attempt by way of negotiation.

"The scribe", he said; "negotiates with the pen, the monk with the sermon, the knight though with the sword. Anyone who wants to venture with me, come; for before the sun has risen five times the ranks of those proud knights will be broken."

Those present considered him to be a dreamer, and nobody followed his banner. "Good," he said; "then I must attempt it alone so that the honour will come to those who deserve it." He assembled his own men and led them to a steep hill where they could look over the number of the enemy. "Do you see there," he now began; "the hordes who want to cause the shame for our fatherland of receiving laws from them? I want to scatter them apart, like the wind scatters the dust when it passes over the roads. Wait here for three days, on the fourth it will happen!"

The Prussian knights saw this little handful of men and did not know how they should interpret it. "Is it the vanguard of a greater might," they asked amongst each other; "or have the knights on the borders united against us? We must have news before we undertake something."

Now envoys were sent out to all the castles where they suspected they would find loyal adherents, in order to obtain certainty from them. They learnt the entire sequence of events and the adventurous plan of the foreigners, and could barely decide to treat the matter just with some seriousness.

On the third day Gottfried sent a herald to them and had them asked whether they wanted to obligingly vacate the border or intended to await his attack. If they decided for the former, then they should begin the withdrawal early in the morning; for in the case that they still stood in the old place at the sixth hour, then they would see him in the middle amongst them.

They heard the words of the herald with scorn. The leader answered the request with, "Tell he who he sent you that we will await him in this place, for we are curious to see up close such a hero as your lord appears to be."

The herald returned with this answer. Gottfried said, "It will happen as I announced in advance!"

The next day towards the sixth hour the Prussian warriors were still camped at the same place, and abandoning themselves without fear to their games and delights. Gottfried went within himself and gazed at the movements which he was to make. Everything stood clearly before him. He went down the slope calmly with his men, separated them into two groups and said, "One group remains here, with the other I will fall on the enemy, and when they take flight and do not know where to go, they will run into the hands of those who remained here and will be destroyed. The power does not lie in the size of the numbers, but rather in that they hold together and penetrate to the centre."

He now approached his opponents. They gazed at him the way you watch someone passing by who is of little importance and offers at most material for laughter. At once his horse flew, the others behind him, and like the light penetrates through the open window and quickly illuminates the whole room, just as quickly had they spread through the horde and marked their appearance with death and wounding. There was no order anymore amongst the enemy horde; each fled individually to the hill on which Gottfried had previously stood, and ran, as he had said, right into the hands of the group placed there. In three hours all was done, and Gottfried called out, "For the second time you, eternal power, have revealed yourself to me; see me in the dust before you, you great, strong, almighty God!" He sank to his knees and lingered for a long time in his inner-being in order to rejoice there and suitably give thanks.

This event caused a great sensation. The German knights were ashamed to have treated their helper so basely. The Prussian allies, however, were full of fury and decided to make good this loss again in another way.

They sent secret envoys out to the German knights on the border in order to enquire as to which would like to be of help to them for a plan which they were devising for revenge and as a precaution and from which they expected repayment for the loss they had suffered. Those namely who would undertake it to get out of the way that adventurer, as they called Gottfried, they promised a gleaming reward and at the same time also a share in all the conquests which they would make in Germany. The knight Kurt von L..u..gl, an avaricious man, was blinded by the offer and promised to soon have Gottfried snared and to do to him as they wished.

He sent an envoy to Gottfried and had him asked to make his way to his castle and to have a rest there after such a brilliant victory. Gottfried followed the invitation and went with his men to L..u..gl's castle. Kurt indeed suggested it would be sufficient to have the knight alone with himself, the men would be distributed amongst the villages. But they declared that they would not be parted from their lord and would rather make do with the least. L..u..gl put up with it and thought, "If I just first have him in my castle, then he is my prisoner, and my ruse will perhaps succeed all the more certainly if his people are under my eyes."

Three days passed amidst festive delights and close conversations. In the night between the third and the fourth day Gottfried had a vision. He saw the guard which stood before his chamber creep in to place a spear to his chest in order to put it right through him. But at the same moment the weapon broke and Gottfried heard the words, "He stands outside!" He enquired for a few moments within himself and was quickly resolved. He went before the door, recognised the guard from the vision, tore the spear from his hands and broke it. "Go," he said; "and tell your knight, I need no guard, but he should give up his intention, otherwise it will reflect on him."

The guard was as if destroyed. The mercenary confessed everything and asked for mercy. "Leave me," Gottfried commanded, "and do not become a sinner a second time, or you will get what you deserve."

The man left. But Gottfried recognised more and more the powers of the inner life which connected with God and dealt in his clear advice.

A tumult occurred in the castle as if a revolt had broken out. Everybody hurried to their weapons without actually knowing why. In this tumult the lord of the castle had the gates of the castle hurriedly opened and flew in the pitch-black night from there as if death were on his heels. The guard had come to him and had reported the incident with Gottfried. But instead of composing himself, his guilty conscience overcame him, and he was the one who called the garrison to arms without showing himself.

When day had already broken, Gottfried went to the castle's courtyard in order to learn what had happened, for he had heard the tumult of the armed men. The castle warden gave him the news that his knight had gone and tasked him with providing for the guests. Gottfried asked, "Who are you?"

Warden: "The castle's warden."
Gottfried: "Of what class?"
Warden: "A noble."
Gottfried: "And your knight?"
Warden: "Likewise."
Gottfried: "I cannot think it, for a noble should not have been capable of acting so ignobly."
Warden: "I am also of the opinion."
Gottfried: "And your knight?"
Warden: "Will receive the punishment and I fear, this time he will not escape."
Gottfried: "When the twelfth hour, calculated from now, has passed, you will have a sign that what was said here has happened."

Gottfried left the castle and camped in a village in order to be closer to the Prussian knights; for he foresaw that they were not letting up, but rather would apply themselves with doubled force.

Around the fifth hour of night a messenger came from L..u..gl's castle and brought the news that the knight had taken his own life. Horror gripped all the inhabitants, and you did not know where you should take counsel.

The castle warden hurried to Gottfried with this news and asked him to accept the estate.

Gottfried: "Are children present?"
Warden: "Two sons."
Gottfried: "Where are they?"
Warden: "It is not known. The father sent them away out of fear they might strive after their inheritance."
Gottfried: "Have them searched for."
Warden: "No trace is known of them."
Gottfried: "Then I will look after their discovery. You, noble warden, take over the administration of their property until they themselves appear. I will have you discharge your

duties in the name of German chivalry. Swear to me to be true and to preserve the entrusted estate as if it were your own property."

The castle warden raised his hand and made the oath.

***

New Battle

After a few days they again saw Prussian men who belonged to the hordes of the already well-known order of knights. Gottfried made the German castle lords aware of it and had them asked whether they were now resolved to take part in the battle which would soon arise again. They consulted. A few voices rose for the battle. Sir Gebhard von B..hl declared that it was shameful to always give way to the enemy. A young warrior from Sch..b..l had already brought them to shame. He was resolved either to destroy his knight's coat of arms or to fight like it befitted a German.

This speech was accepted and all called out, "To battle!" They hurried home from the gathering full of brave enthusiasm for Germany's affair, gathered their mercenaries and men, and before fifteen days had passed, a terrible army stood quickly there.

Now it was asked who should lead them. Most of the voices fell to Gottfried. Gebhard von B..hl, however, countered, "By no means, noble knights, do I consider this to be fitting; I suggest that he not fight, but rather begrudge us making good again what has been neglected. If we do not succeed, then we will ask him to lead us and to battle for us a second time. One of us will be the leader with the first attack, and whomsoever the lot falls to, I swear him obedience in advance."

Everybody considered this suggestion to be good and Gebhard von B..hl was elected as leader.

After five days the armies found themselves opposite each other. The outcome was uncertain, for both armies were numerous and each full of lust for battle to restore their honour. On the sixth day the battle began with the rising of the sun. Luck seemed sometimes to lean here, sometimes there. Suddenly the grandmaster of the Prussian order of knights appeared on the battlefield with fresh warriors and the Germans began to give way. Gottfried saw this turn and could not yet assist.

The Prussian warriors surged forward more and more forcibly and the Germans who escaped the pursuit threw themselves into the nearby castles and fortresses. "Where now is that Gottfried?", the victorious grandmaster asked as he rode across the battlefield that evening; "The one who frightened you so much recently? Do you think he did not fight with them today? It would be strange if he remained calm at the misfortune of his own people. Your tale was a fairy tale, which today has proven."

The Germans were discouraged. Gebhard von B..hl himself handed over the command to Gottfried and said, "You were already chosen in advance. If you can avert the consequences of our loss for Germany, then do so; but if it is not possible for you, then I want to enter a monastery and forget that I ever wielded a sword." Gottfried offered the bowed man his hand, and said, "You are not at fault for that which has happened, a higher fate reigns here. But pull yourself together. Before two times fifty hours have flown by, no Prussian will be seen here anymore."

He went the next day to L..u..gl's castle in order to look over the area from its battlements. The victors were swarming around wildly in order to take still more prisoners. "How will it turn out?", he asked; "Good!", rang out the answer. "I must believe and proceed to act," he thought, "for two times fifty hours are soon over."

He hurried to his men and gave them the task of going around the castles close by in order to get hold of more fighters. It happened, and the next day, before the sun went down, a quite large group had already assembled around him.

"It is enough!", he said. "Not the number, but the spirit gives the strength. Tomorrow it shall begin, and before the sun has reached its highest position, the victory will have been decided for us. Be brave! Anyone who has trust will need no sword, but anyone who approaches the enemy with doubt my shield cannot protect. In the morning, when the new day shows itself, gather here again so that you hear how everything shall happen."

New Battle

He soon went to bed and for the first time he gave the command they should wake him in the morning. "The external nature", he said, "is horrified by the coming day, I must give it refreshment. The spirit will quickly decide when the moment demands."

The next morning the men has assembled at the appointed time. He spoke in the following way to them. "When the bell tolls from that tower which I will show you, then ride forwards. The enemy's main force has camped down by the river. There is our first place to entice them to attack. They will not come. Then we will go upriver and when we have put a thousand paces behind us, we will reach the ford which will serve for us to cross. Now note well what I now say. You who stand to my left, move forwards on the road as if you want to draw the enemy into the countryside and do not stop until the noise of the fleeing men enters your ears — then turn and do what the duty of a warrior is. You who are to my right, you will charge with me at that group which intoxicated by fame allows us to get close in order to destroy us all the better. Follow me there and I tell you, they will flee before we have properly hit them, for the powers of the spirit go before us as warriors who are invincible and bring disgrace on every enemy."

It happened as he said. They took up position by the river; the enemy, however, mocked them. They went a thousand paces upriver and encountered the ford; the crossed unhindered and divided there. The enemy watched it all calmly and neither sword nor lance stirred. Now Gottfried's battle steed reared up and his chest rose higher. "The king calls!", it sounded from his mouth; "According to him the victory is ours!!"

As quickly as an arrow flies from the bow, he rode towards the troops equipped for battle. His men sprang after him. His sword made a path and parted the limbs as if he had lightning in his hand. Confusion arose amongst the attacked before they were properly set to defend. Only individuals still sought to fight in order to bring order into the ranks again, but even these lost the courage, for the leader of the Germans was everywhere with his sword of flames and many thought his eyes were already bringing death. They all took flight and strove to reach the road inland, but there they fell into the hands of the group that had gone on ahead and saw with horror death behind them and in front of them. Soon the victory was complete and when the sun was approaching its highest point, you saw only dead and captured Prussian warriors.

"Hallelujah, to the God of strength!", Gottfried called out and everybody joined in his jubilation.

The news of this victory had spread quickly through the region. Gebhard von B..hl came that same day to Gottfried and said, "I would bend my knee before you if I did not consider it to be sinful. You are the saviour of Germany. What honour can reward you suitably?"

Gottfried: "Leave me alone! Do not seduce my ears with words of flattery! Without my teacher, what would I be? Without my mother, who gave him to me, what would I be capable of? God alone is almighty, God alone is omnipresent, and in his knowledge lies the power before which all enemies tremble. Help me praise him, noble man! Shout to me for evermore that it is only he who is capable of everything, so that the giddiness of my fortune does not bewitch me and I dedicate myself to what is not human, but rather divine."

B..hl: "I admire you! Admire your talk just as much as your deeds. Such humility with so much magnificence! Such sacrifice with so much strength! Noble young man, I cannot grasp it and would not believe it, if I had not seen and heard it myself."

Gottfried: "Enough of these words. We are freed from our enemy; let us rejoice this and leave the honour alone to the one who deserves it: God!"

***

Gottfried's Homecoming

After a few days, when Gottfried had made the necessary arrangements with the knights, and the two sons of the knight L..n..gl had been drawn out of their hiding, he assembled his men around him and said, "Here the battles are over, at home though there is great hardship; hence let us go there."

There much had also changed in fact. The fury of the parties had risen to an extreme on account of the doubled possession of the imperial throne. Bavaria had all the cities for itself, but Austria had the knighthood. This division gave material for frictions which were more harmful to the fatherland than the most violent battle. The stirred up citizens, after they had taken up arms, knew no bounds anymore and marked their marches with fire and murder. The knights locked themselves up in their castles and a uniting of their forces was not to be thought of anymore because each shied from leaving his property in order to not deliver it into the hands of the cities.

Amidst incessant battles Gottfried reached his home and entered the castle of his birth to the joy of his mother and his father, who had meanwhile return home from the field, and amidst the jubilation of all the castle residents. You would attempt in vain to describe the feelings which he and his family felt when they saw each other again and greeted one another full of heartfelt love.

The father had heard of Gottfried's deeds and could not believe it; his mother sank to her knees before everyone and thanked God to have such a son; indeed everyone considered him to be a chosen one, sent to them for their salvation and for the rescue of the fatherland which had been afflicted with terrible storms.

"Where is my teacher?", Gottfried asked. "He is gone;" his mother answered. "He declared his work was complete and left us in order to extol his divine doctrine in another place." At this news Gottfried chest rose and a tear entered his eye. "For him," he said, "I have yearned like for a saint, for that which he gave me is a sacred thing against which all the treasures and riches of the world are only dust."

***

The Townsmen

Now he consulted with his father over Germany's position in order to remedy the nuisance which had gotten out of hand. "It must not remain like this!", he said; "To the tradesman belongs his business, and to the knight the sword; if the townsfolk and the countrymen take up weapons, then the sources of nourishment will be interrupted and famine and plague will be the afterpains of war. It must change, and before the sun had risen five times something shall already have happened."

His father, who was hearing his power of action from Gottfried himself, handed the castle over to him and appointed him as rightful lord of Er..k..ng. At the same time he decorated him with the order insignia of the German knights or the German Lords, and called upon him to decide and act in future according to his own free will.

"I see the knights are intimidated", Gottfried said; "I want to wake them up from their paralysis so that we will stand with decency opposite the contenders for the imperial crown."

Right the next day he left the castle in order to visit the neighbouring knights and to talk them into a meeting. They did not seem to have the courage, for they gave him evasive answers. "Emperor Ludwig, the Bavarian, is too powerful; he hates the knighthood and hence the cleverest thing is to be calm until the circumstances are favourable again." — "Now then," Gottfried replied, "if you do not have the courage to do something for the fatherland and for the honour of the knighthood, then I will undertake it alone. The power which helped me vanquish those northern fighters will also assist me here where I am as it were forced to fight for my person and the hearth of my house."

He assembled about himself his well-tested troops again, and a number of new warriors who were following the fame of his name, and dispersed the townsmen wherever he encountered them. F...t, that rich town, had acquired an army of mercenaries and, when the town council there learned of Gottfried's intentions, they sent envoys Ludwig's camp and made a request for support and orders of restraint. Both succeeded. Count B..n..rt came at the head of a select troop and conveyed the imperial authority to do everything which was considered good to undertake against the German knights.

Now the slogan was given. The words "War against the knighthood!" had torn all the bonds which still existed between the people and the knights. Many order members cursed Gottfried's carelessness in having the matter taken so far and silently sent envoys to the Bavarian main camp in order to offer their complete subjection. "The dice has been cast," Gottfried said; "through hesitation the evil will just get worse and our glorious order, formed for the protection of the emperors and their lands, will lose one member after another until it dissolves. Quick action alone can yet avert the evil."

He moved against F...t and called upon the citizenry to lay down their weapons and go about their business. The herald was mocked. He repeated the demand twice. The third time, instead of any answer, an enormous army advanced towards him in order to destroy him with one blow.

"It has come as I saw;" Gottfried said calmly to his men. "Now listen to me! When I call you, follow me. When I ride slowly, then do so too, but when I charge, wherever it be, then raise a noise as if thousands of legions were advancing. Take note, it will go well."

He now rode slowly forwards. The opponents saw it and were uncertain whether he was approaching so calmly to parley or for battle. Then he steered to the left, towards a meadow where a troop of riders had positioned themselves. Then he once more took a different direction and all as calmly as if he were seeking a lost gem. Count B..n..rt, who was also present with his Bavarians, finally called out full of annoyance, "That is a madman who is pulling our leg with his slow movements! Fall on him so that the play comes to an end!" Hardly had he spoken than he advanced with his men in order to be the first to strike a blow on that strange person. This was the sign which Gottfried had seen in the spirit. And now he rose up on his battle steed as if he wanted fly over the heads of his enemies. Before the count could think, he was lying on the ground, his soldiers wanted to rush to his aid, but the lances and swords of Gottfried's warriors were shining as if it were raining fire from heaven. The noise which they made was like a hurricane when it is tearing up walls and houses, and the quickness with which everything happened was so horrifying that the townsmen's knees trembled and the most experienced soldiers lost courage. "Throw your weapons away!", Gottfried shouted when the noise had abated a little, and lances and swords lay on the ground all around.

They all crawled home and did not think again about going to battle. Count B..n..rt, whom the fall had not harmed much, approached Gottfried and asked whether he would treat him as a prisoner or give him his freedom on his word as a knight. "Go wherever you want!", Gottfried replied. "But I tell you this; do not come against me anymore as a warrior, otherwise you will be lost with no hope of rescue!"

After this victory which was decisive for the knighthood's matter, he again made his rounds of the neighbouring castles to collect adherents for the preservation of German arrangements. This time they listened to him and the offer was made unanimously to establish a large chapter of the order in order to consult over all the circumstances of the fatherland and the knighthood.

Emperor Ludwig had barely heard of the defeat of the F...t men and the resolve of the knighthood to consult in an order chapter, when he sent envoys to all the regions in order to thwart such a coming together. He did not spare pleas nor threats in order to achieve his aim, but it all fell apart on the unshakeable declaration of Gottfried that he would not put his sword back in its scabbard until such an assembly of knights had taken place.

Ludwig heard this declaration and was close to outlawing him; but his advisors held him back from this step in order to not antagonise the knighthood even more and create in this way a greater following for the Austrians. He let himself be dissuaded this time from his intention, but swore to make use of his right at the first opportunity.

Gottfried was informed of the emperor's intention and advised to be on his guard, but he answered, "Only what is right can happen!" He stuck with that only a general order chapter over the circumstances worrying the fatherland could decide, and continued calling up everybody in order to bring it about. With his victorious troops he repulsed the attacks of the Luxembourgers, cleansed the land of the forays of the towns and thereby turned the imperial might back on itself in that he took the help of the towns away from it.

After half a year the German knighthood finally assembled in N...g, and was as numerous as never before.

***

Order Chapter

It was stirring to see all the brave men to whom Germany had often already owed its survival, and who now themselves were being oppressed by an emperor who did not yet possess the full confirmation of his dignity. The entire land directed its gaze to them and hoped of them that the unravelling of circumstances which restricted everybody for whom their own and the welfare of others lay at heart.

Emperor Ludwig had called together a pugnacious force in order to make a violent attempt to drive the knights of the order apart, but the bold Leopold of Austria, who expected from this meeting a favourable turning for the other emperor, his brother Friedrich, moved to the borders of Bavaria and hindered Ludwig's intentions.

The chapter was opened. Great solemnity and august seriousness reigned in it. The order's grandmaster, the knight Adalbert von M..g..n, dissected in an involved speech the aim of their being there and concluded in the following way.

"The fatherland, because it is ruled by two emperors, is without a leader, for our state's basic law allows only one emperor. The knighthood, as support of him and as defender of his and the land's rights, is made ineffective because it is robbed of its dignity and excluded from consultation of public affairs. Our weapons, so one imagines, are not needed anymore, and one thinks in the future to carry out war with mercenaries and townsmen. If from this project the welfare of the land could arise, then I would not speak against it and would be the first to transform his sword into a ploughshare; but the time has not yet come which allows such an action, when our fatherland is still surrounded all around by neighbours thirsty for conquest, against which you must be constantly equipped. How is this to be demanded of country and townsfolk without bringing hardship and misery amongst all classes! — In this respect and in the power of my rights transmitted by statutory law, I therefore ask the great assembly: is Ludwig of Bavaria the lawful emperor?"

The knights: "No!"

Grandmaster: "Is Friedrich of Austria lawful emperor?"

The knights: "No!"

Grandmaster: "Shall steps be taken for a new imperial election?"

The knights: "Yes!"

Gottfried von Er..k..ng asked for permission to speak, and after it had been given to him, he began.

"I foresee how it will occur. The emperor will remain and a reconciliation will take place between Bavaria and Austria. If this happens, the fatherland will obtain peace and win time to heal the wounds it has received."

The greatest part of those present was against this view. "Ludwig", they said; "has declared himself too loudly against the knighthood and will not conclude any peace with it without it having been completely oppressed beforehand; and hence we remain of our opinion: that only a newly elected emperor can guarantee external and internal peace for the land."

The knight von F..l..au, who was amongst the latter, rose and requested permission to speak. "Why", he began, "want to remain in an uncertain state? Why not seize the nearest means which stand at our command? Gottfried von Er..k..ng has destroyed Germany's enemies, he has opened for us here the paths through all obstacles and distinguished himself from all others through his selflessness and courage. In him is the power and the cleverness to reign; he alone is in the position to defend our rights against anyone, and hence I declare: he should be emperor!"

As if seized by a magic spell the entire gathering called out, "Emperor Gottfried!"

The grandmaster left his elevated seat, placed the order's sword at Gottfried's feet and said, "Wield it for the good of all, you are capable of it. Long live Gottfried, the emperor!"

Gottfried had let everything happen without making a movement; but now he responded, "Not so, noble knights!

Not so, august chapter!" With indescribable emotion he looked upwards and continued in great enthusiasm, "I am standing on the heights of human greatness; Europe, I see, lies at my feet and a power exists in me by which I could dominate it untouched. But it is not the will of my power that I do so. It has led me to these heights in order to show me what it is capable of. I am astonished with humility and reject your request."

All the voices rose against him and made it a duty for him to accept the offered dignity. But he answered, "Tomorrow the news will come of Friedrich and Ludwig's reconciliation; then the government, even if under two names, will be under only one sceptre. Wait until this news comes, and then consider what is to be done in future."

It was decided to assemble again the next day. The news of the reconciliation came, and since Gottfried stuck to his decision, they entered negotiations with both emperors in order to clear up the affairs and circumstances of the order. Gottfried himself undertook the negotiations, and everything turned out to the satisfaction of both parties.

Emperor Ludwig, who had heard of Gottfried's deeds and his declining of the imperial dignity, suddenly felt like getting to know such an exceptional man and summoned him to visit his court where he showed him great attention and honour. Gottfried lingered for two weeks there and took his leave amidst honest assurances of imperial grace and favour.

He lived for many years in his own family circle, loved by his own, treasured and honoured by all who knew him, whilst, where it was necessary, he strove to promote the fortunes of his neighbours and the fatherland.

His coat of arms exists with a few alterations still amongst his descendants, and vouches for the truth of his sublime virtues.

***

Overview

Anyone who read in the cited examples of attained spiritual freedom the story of Gottfried von Er..k..ng first would think themselves transported into a fairy tale world where the most unbound fantasy is creating and describing events; but anyone who follows the content of the book from beginning to end attentively is forced to the conclusion that, if the first phenomena are true, the last must also be.

In order to make this clearer for the reader, we will place the above examples opposite one another so as to describe their relationship to one another more certainly.

The first thing to which the content of this book points is the magnetism. Its highest stage is involuntary clairvoyance. We have not portrayed this condition historically because it belongs under the absolute knowledge of the day.

Clairvoyance without being asleep and without being magnetised is indeed not a new condition, but rather a freer condition where the healthy person has complete consciousness of the same phenomena as the somnambulist. The apprentice joiner delivers an example of it.

A different form of invisible powers in the nature of the human are intuitions and dreams. It is a lower degree than clairvoyance because the impressions are often wild and chaotic, but they arise from the same source and are native in all families. Herdtmann's mother was driven by such influences to the rescue of her son.

Herdtmann himself went away from the accidental impression and passed over to the theory, made the state of clairvoyance into his free possession in which he began his researches and raised it to a science. He shared his teachings with two students. The first, a mathematician, considered in these new circumstances alone the conditions of life to be fulfilled, and L...h established on them his philosophy which he declared to be stemming from eternity and alone to be true.

The life of the last was almost a constant clairvoyance and the images which his inner life showed him were in the end the servants of his will whereby he healed illnesses and discovered the most hidden things.

Much more is to be said about it, but at present we refer to the doctrine of Herdtmann which he shared with his students, indeed concisely, but frankly.

In the thirteenth century we see a phenomenon which rests on the same laws and arises from the characteristics of a free clairvoyance. In that time the exercise of power applied more than all knowing, and hence the Cardinal C...h and the chaplain to whom Gottfried was given as student seemed to have worked exclusively in it to fathom the inner characteristics of a Joshua, Gideon, Samson, etc., and to increase the strength of belief in the phenomena of clairvoyance to the point where all obstacles vanish and the inner free will vanquishes everything which stands in its way.

L...h is an example of a free knowing, Gottfried of a free power; but both are brothers of one and the same light which sends its rays wherever the will of the human directs.

This light shines at all times and in all zones, and gives itself to be recognised in its entire fullness by everyone who seeks it with zeal and effort. Means to it are given above and thus we present to everyone who has the courage for it the key, and wish that they may succeed in unlocking the spirit world with it.

***

Other works by Johann Baptist Krebs (originally published in German under the pseudonym of J. B. Kerning) translated and published by K A Nitz

Paths to Immortality
Based on the Undeniable Powers
of Human Nature

Christianity
or
God and Nature Only One
Through the Word

The Missionaries
The Path to the Teaching Profession
of Christianity

The Principles of the Bible

The Freemason

Wisdom of the Orient

And by his student Karl Kolb

The Rebirth, the inner true life, or
how do humans become blessed?
In accordance with the words of the sacred scripture
and the laws of thinking

www.ingramcontent.com/pod-product-compliance
Lightning Source LLC
Chambersburg PA
CBHW022104160426
43198CB00008B/346